Jesus said he came to give every single person who followed him a "rich and satisfying life." (John 10:10, NLT). Why don't more of us, as Christ-followers, experience the fullness of life Jesus offers? One big reason is we aren't adequately aware of the tricks, weapons, and tools of the enemy. "The thief's purpose is to steal, kill and destroy" (John 10:10, NLT).

The spiritual realm is real and primal. What happens in that realm affects our degree of aliveness, now and forever. In *Caught Between Heaven and Hell*, Don Stewart gives helpful insights into what the "life-robber" is up to, and the resources God has given us to be faithful overcomers. This is more than theology and theory to Don. He lives this stuff. I've seen him help countless people become free to live fully. I'm excited to think that through this book even more will come to live in victory and abundance.

KEN JOHNSON, FORMER LEAD PASTOR OF WESTSIDE CHURCH, BEND OR

Caught Between Heaven and Hell is an amazingly thorough and practical read. Don Stewart has provided the Christian with a vital tool with which to engage and successfully confront the realm of darkness. Many books have been written on spiritual warfare and healing, but few have been able to answer a good many of the questions that arise, such as: *Why is this so? or How does that work?* C.S. Lewis spoke of two dangers: one being an unhealthy interest in the demonic; the other, being oblivious to its workings. This book has the rare quality of balancing factual with applicable. The reader will truly know why there is a need to understand the spiritual war zone each of us face, while being given the tools to successfully and victoriously respond. If you are looking for a resource that can help others who are losing ground to the kingdom of darkness, or you are seeking to be personally equipped to live life in a spiritual war zone, make this an essential part of your reading. Stewart has provided the church with what I believe will be a classic and helpful study, for those new to their faith in Christ as well as those who have known him for years.

CHRIS HAYWARD, PASTOR; PRESIDENT OF CLEANSING STREAM MINISTRIES

Pastor Don Stewart's new book, *Caught Between Heaven and Hell,* provides a biblically based prescription for the soul. Don provides understanding as to why we can suffer the spiritual, psychological, and even physical challenges coming from the real battle in this world, which happens in our own mind. As a Christian and a licensed physician assistant in family medicine and psychotherapy for over thirty years, I find this book helpful both professionally and personally. Thank you, Don.

SHELLEY MAURICE-MAIER, PA-C, AUTHOR OF *THE SOUL FACTOR*

Caught Between Heaven and Hell details the process of restoring ourselves in the Truth that brings freedom. I have used this process in ministry and in my professional counseling practice; in every case, God has stepped in to transform rm a life. Pastors, counselors, intercessors, and disciplers will benefit from its in-depth discussion of the "weapons of our warfare." I sense the Lord will use this book to equip the helper and heal the brokenhearted. I am honored and delighted to recommend it.

SUSAN K. GOODMAN, MA, LPC,CLC, BEND, OR

Every Christ follower must think through the issue this book presents. Scripture makes it clear that we are involved in a spiritual battle. However, the practical effects and personal preparation required for victory are often overlooked. Don Stewart has blended the disciplines of biblical study, thorough research, and practical experience to ready every believer for battle. This book will heighten your awareness of the conflict which rages, while bringing renewed confidence in the victory already won.

LARRY R. SPOUSTA, DISTRICT SUPERVISOR NORTH PACIFIC DISTRICT OF FOURSQUARE CHURCHES

Whether you have been a Christian for a matter of days or a lifetime, Don Stewart's work in *Caught Between Heaven and Hell* will be a treasure chest you will go back to over and over again. His heart comes through on every page. Stewart carefully weaves a tapestry of truths from the Word of

God and other sources to present the reader with a clear understanding of the nature of the battle we are engaged in. The authenticity of a changed life will speak to those searching to understand what it means to walk out the freedom and healing

Jesus purchased through his blood. This book will delight believers who have found themselves asking the tough questions about spiritual realities. Stewart examines the big picture and helps believers see the necessity of both healing and walking in truth, to live an overcoming life. I look forward to challenging our body of believers to read this amazing exposition on spiritual warfare.

DEBBIE SAYOVITZ, FAMILY AND INNER HEALING PASTOR
EPICENTRE CHURCH, PASADENA CA

Don Stewart's new book, *Caught Between Heaven and Hell*, makes a significant contribution to our understanding of spiritual health and freedom. Don writes from a background of theological education, pastoral ministry, and counseling experience, along with a broad-spectrum awareness of culture and how it impacts our thinking and behavior.

This very readable book is filled with accessible information and written for practical application. The explanation of footholds and strongholds is clear and understandable, the practical action steps for dealing with past issues and present challenges are straightforward, and the section on staying free is especially helpful. You'll appreciate Don's thoroughness in providing notes from his journal, a list of additional resources, and well thought-out discussion questions for use in groups and in counseling settings.

JIM STEPHENS, PASTOR, MISSIONARY, AND AUTHOR OF
GRACENOTES

Introduction

First, let me tell you a story.

Once upon a time, there were people who lived in a physical, space-time cosmos. These people could see, touch, feel, and measure just about everything in the planet they lived on.. In this story, there was another (parallel) spiritual realm that was just as real as the physical world. The spiritual realm also was occupied by living, sentient beings. Most of those in the physical world were unaware of the spiritual realm and lived their lives as though it didn't exist.

To make things even more complicated, some of the beings in the spiritual world were evil and wanted to hurt the people who lived in the physical world in any way they could. These evil beings wanted to do this because they had rebelled against the ruler and creator of both worlds.

The evil beings had the ability to suggest ideas and thoughts to the people they wanted to hurt without their realizing that the thoughts came from a source other than their own minds. Over time, these evil beings were able to convince most of these people that there was no spiritual world; or, if there was one, it was not at all like the one that really did exist. This allowed the evil beings to get most of the people in the physical world to believe things about themselves, about their world, and about the spiritual world (if there was one) that were not true. By doing this, they got the people who believed their lies to behave in ways that destroyed and polluted both their world and the people who lived in it. People found themselves in bondage to the habits, addictions, and other self-destructive behaviors established in their lives because of their mistaken beliefs. The evil ones even got many of the people to cooperate with them in their rebellion against the creator.

The creator knew what was going on in the worlds he had made and was very sad about all that was happening because he loved those in both worlds and had originally created them to be in close relationship with himself. He had given all the beings in both worlds the right of self-determination and, even though he could have, he had decided not to over-rule their free will. This free will is what had allowed them not only to rebel but also to return his love if they chose to. The creator was really in a tough spot because he was both loving and just. He couldn't just ignore the rebellion and forgive those who rebelled without justice being served – so he came up with a plan. The stakes were high because the penalty for rebellion was death.

The creator revealed the truth about what was really going on in the physical world to many people. These people told others. Some believed them and others didn't. Many of the messengers the creator sent were killed by those who chose not to believe their message. Finally, the creator decided to bring the message to the world himself and to pay the penalty for the rebellion himself so that anyone who would believe the truth and accept his free gift of pardon could be adopted as sons and daughters into his family and eternally enjoy the life they were created to live in the first place.

As you may have already suspected, this is a very abbreviated version of a true story. It explains why this world is in such a mess and lets us know that there is a happy ending to the story for those who want one.

Is this story really true? If it is, there is a big problem for those of us who are still living in this world. We have all been exposed to the lies of the evil ones since we were children. How do we recognize the lies? Once we have, what can we do about them? What are the consequences of these lies in our lives? How do we keep from being deceived by new lies? How can we get free from the bondage to the habits, addictions, and other self-destructive behaviors established in our lives because of these mistaken beliefs? Once we've gotten free, how can we stay free? This book has been written to answer these questions and many more.

In his famous speech "*The Weight of Glory*", C. S. Lewis concluded his remarks with these thoughts:

> "… It is a serious thing to live in a society of possible gods and goddesses, to remember that the dullest and most uninteresting person you can talk to may one day be a creature which, if you saw it now, you would be strongly tempted to worship, or else a horror and a corruption such as you now meet, if at all, only in a nightmare. All day long we are, in

some degree, helping each other to one or the other of these dimensions. …There are no ordinary people. You have never talked to a mere mortal. Nations, cultures, arts, civilizations, - these are mortal, and their life is to ours as the life of a gnat. But it is immortals whom we joke with, work with, marry, snub, and exploit – immortal horrors or everlasting splendours… ."(add citation)

The things that we think are facts, are true – our worldview - determines our decisions and our behaviors and, cumulatively, they determine our ultimate fate - either as "immortal horrors or everlasting splendors". Someone has said, "Life is not for sissies." Both good things and bad happen to all of us. Some have it much worse than others. How we respond to the things that happen in life determines which direction we are moving – toward becoming a horror or a splendor.

This book explains why we find our lives and our relationships with others and with God in such a mess and what we can do about it. It is a book for people who know they haven't always made the best decisions or behaved in the best possible way – people who are willing to take an honest look at their life – people who are willing to make adjustments in their lives based on reality and truth. Maybe things are going pretty well right now. Maybe you are experiencing some of the consequences from earlier decisions you wish you hadn't made. Either way, we can begin moving in the right direction as we begin making decisions based on reality and truth. This book is divided into three sections: The Truth, Getting Free, and Staying Free. (Does this sentence belong here?)

John the Baptist said, "A man can receive nothing unless it has been given him from heaven"[1]. The apostle Paul said virtually the same thing to the Corinthian church[2]. One of the gifts I have been given is the ability to take insights and understandings from many different sources and combine them in ways that help others see a bigger, more complete picture of truth; to more clearly see relationships and make associations that might not have otherwise been made. This is not a source of "new truth" but a combination of existing truths – sometimes in new ways. By the way, no one has a corner on all the truth except God Himself. The Bible says that what *we* know now is partial and incomplete, like seeing a reflection in a poor mirror[3]. There is another thing we need to know about truth. It won't do us any good to know what truth is unless we are willing to use and apply the truth we do know. Growth in our knowledge and understanding of truth requires that we use and apply the truth we already have[4].

I have been a life-long learner. I will not always be able to remember the source of everything I will share. I will do my best to credit sources whenever I know what they are. Appendix A is a list of recommended Reading. It will include most of these sources referenced and many others.

I have been a pastor for more than 40 years. Over this time, I have worked with hundreds of people trying to help them deal with the problems in their lives. In the earlier years, perhaps 20% of those who came for help actually seemed to receive the help they needed and be able to apply it in their lives without needing to come back for more help. Then I began to understand and share more and more of the truths provided in this book, to teach them to understand and apply these truths for themselves. Over the past several years, more than 80% of those who have come for help have understood and have begun to successfully apply these truths in their lives without needing to come back for more help. Many have begun helping others in the same way. As a result, they have been able to experience more successful, happy, and joyful lives.

It has been said that you can't give away what you haven't truly experienced in your own life. As I have applied these truths in my own life, I have come to a degree of freedom, peace, and a sense of God's presence that I scarcely would have believed possible just a few years ago. I sense God saying to me, "You ain't seen nothin' yet!" He is saying the same thing to you.

REALITY

What is "reality"? Webster's New World Dictionary says that reality is, "the quality or fact of being real; ...true to life..." Some people believe that the stories Christians believe are simply myths – fantastic stories that may hint at one truth or another – but simply stories that are not based on reality.

There are many who will tell you and truly believe that there is only one reality – our physical world – that only what we can see, hear, taste, smell, touch, and measure is truly real. Many of these and others will tell you that there is no way to really know truth. They'll tell you that there are all kinds and shades of truth and that all "truth" is relative – that "true" truth (i.e., absolute truth) is unknowable. Now, if we accept the premise that reality is limited to only what can be measured, then we would have to accept that a "spiritual" world (if one exists) is simply not part of any reality that we can know. If, on the other hand, you are willing to agree that reality could possibly involve much more that we can measure with physical instruments, then you'll need another source of information that can tell you more about reality. The information provided by that source would have to come from outside our current physical reality. That is exactly what the Bible claims to be - information from and about a reality beyond our physical world.[1] The Bible is a compilation of 66 books that were written over a period of more than 1500 years by inspired writers. These people may or may not have realized that they were inspired by the being who created the physical cosmos and who exists in a spiritual world separate from our physical world and yet is capable of interacting with it.

C. S. Lewis said:

> The heart of Christianity is a myth which is also a fact. The old myth of the dying God, without ceasing to be myth, comes down from the heaven of legend and imagination to the earth of history. It happens--at a particular date, in a particular place, followed by definable historical consequences. We pass

from a Balder or an Osiris, dying nobody knows when or where, to a historical Person crucified (it is all in order) under Pontius Pilate. By becoming fact it does not cease to be myth: that is the miracle. I suspect that men have sometimes derived more spiritual sustenance from myths they did not believe than from the religion they professed. To be truly Christian we must both assent to the historical fact and also receive the myth (fact though it has become) with the same imaginative embrace which we accord to all myth. The one is hardly more necessary than the other.[2]

John Eldredge has recognized the same truth but put it in another way:

We live in a far more dramatic, far more dangerous Story than we ever imagined. The reason we love [stories like] The Chronicles of Narnia or Star Wars or The Matrix or The Lord of the Rings is because they are telling us something about our lives that we never, ever get on the evening news, or from most pulpits. They are reminding us of the Epic we are created for. This is the sort of tale you've fallen into. How would you live differently if you believed it to be true?[3]

In the 1999 motion picture *The Matrix,* Thomas Anderson, a.k.a. Neo, is a young computer programmer by day and an illegal hacker by night. In his search for information about something called the Matrix, he is unexpectedly summoned to a suspenseful meeting with Morpheus, a mysterious and intriguing stranger who is about to offer him the chance to see what is really going on:

Morpheus: "I imagine that right now you're feeling a bit like Alice, tumbling down the rabbit hole."

Neo: "You could say that."

Morpheus: "Let me tell you why you're here. You're here because you know something. What you know you can't explain. But you feel it. You've felt it your entire life—that there's something wrong with the world. You don't know what it is but it's there—like a splinter in your mind, driving you mad. It is this feeling that has brought you to me. Do you know what I'm talking about?

Neo: "The Matrix?"

Morpheus: "Do you want to know what it is?"

Neo: (He slowly nods his head yes.)

Morpheus: "The Matrix is everywhere. It is all around us, even now in this very room. You can see it when you look out your window or when you turn on your television. You can feel it when you go to work, when you go to church, when you pay your taxes. It is the world that has been pulled over your eyes to blind you from the truth."

Neo: "What truth?"

Morpheus: "That you are a slave, Neo. Like everyone else, you were born into bondage, into a prison that you cannot smell or taste or touch, a prison for your mind. Unfortunately, no one can be told what the Matrix is. You have to see it for yourself."

(Morpheus then stretches out both of his hands, palms up. In each hand is a large capsule, one red, one blue.)

Morpheus: "This is your last chance. After this, there is no turning back. You take the blue pill, the story ends. You wake up in your bed and you believe whatever you want to believe. You take the red pill, you stay in Wonderland and I show you how deep the rabbit hole goes."

Many of us can relate to Neo. Deep down we sense that something is off. Things don't quite add up, but we're not sure how or why. We need to know more about what is going on in our world. We need a clearer perspective, or else we will misunderstand much of what is happening to us and what can be done about it. It is just a guess – but, I think both 'pills' could have just as well been placeboes. What was actually being offered was the opportunity to make a commitment, make a decision to discover what truth really was.

This book offers you a choice similar to the one offered Neo. The "red pill" I am offering you involves learning the truth about spiritual reality and your unique place in that reality. I freely admit that I am biased. I believe that every effect has a cause and that the only exception to that statement is God Himself. If this statement is true, this means that God existed before, outside, and separate from the cosmos. So, if we are going to know anything about God, It will be only because He has chosen to reveal Himself to us. I believe he has done this in two primary ways: through nature (His creation) and, primarily, through the Bible.

I'm going to tell you what the Bible has to say to us about the spiritual world and how it relates to our physical world. I have chosen the Bible as my source because I believe that it is the only *authoritative* source of this information. C. S. Lewis wrote, "Do not be scared by the word 'authority'. Believing things on authority only means believing them because you have been told them by someone you think trustworthy. Ninety-nine percent of the things you believe are believed on authority."[4] I won't be trying to defend what the Bible says or defend the truth of what it has to say. There is no shortage of fine books that speak to these issues. One of the best books I've read that speaks to these issues is Kenneth Samples' book *A World of Difference*[5] because Samples combines truth from a wide range of sources and explains things in a down-to-earth way. Several references are included in Appendix A for those who would like to pursue this kind of information.

Can you imagine what it would be like to have to put a 1000 piece puzzle together without a picture of what it is supposed to look like when completed? In a way, that is a lot like the situation we find ourselves in when we try to make sense of what has happened in the past and all that is currently happening in our lives and the world around us. It's tough enough when you have the picture. It seems almost impossible when you don't. This chapter will give you an overview of what the Bible says the big picture of physical and spiritual reality looks like, the situation we find ourselves in, and what we can do about it.

The Bible says that "In the beginning, God created the heavens and the earth...and the Spirit of God was hovering over the waters"[6] Someone called "God" existed before the "beginning" and he "created". The Bible says that everything that was created was made out of what was not visible.[7] He pre-existed and did what He did from outside our space and time. It would be easy to get off on sidetracks and conflicts by discussing how and when these things happened. Again, there is no shortage of books that discuss these issues. Several references are included in Appendix A for those who would like to know more about creation.

The first two chapters of Genesis summarize what was included in this process. It says "Let us make man in our image, in our likeness, and let them rule ... So, God created man in his image... male and female he created them."[8] The Bible uses the phrase "in the beginning" one other place: "In the beginning was the Word, and the Word was with God, and the Word was God. He was with God in the beginning. Through him all things were made; without him nothing was made that has been made."[9] The Bible makes it clear that this "Word" who was with God and was God is Jesus Christ. "The Word became flesh and lived for a while among us. We have seen his glory, the glory of the one and only Son, who came from the Father, full of grace and truth."[10] In these few verses, we are introduced to God the Father, God the Holy Spirit, and God the Son; three persons yet one God. That is why the Bible correctly records that God said let "us" make man in "our" image.

In chapter two and three of Genesis, we are introduced to the Garden of Eden, the temptation of Adam and Eve by a talking "serpent", the disobedience (sin) of Adam and Eve, the consequences of their sin, and their removal from the garden. Genesis doesn't record God's creation of a talking snake so there is more to this story than has been explained so far. To quote John Eldredge, "It feels like we have walked into a movie an hour after it started." It is tough to figure out what is going on and where we are in the story. By the way, when you want answers about what the Bible says in one place, you can almost always find the answers by allowing the Bible to explain itself by finding other places where the same subject is discussed. We are told, for example, that the "serpent" was a created being[12] 1 called Satan or the Devil[11]. Who is God? What is He up to? Who is this Satan? Why is he contradicting God and trying to get Adam and Eve in trouble with God? Are there other created beings? So, what is the back-story here?

Good answers to all these questions could take several books to answer completely. Our goal is not to answer these questions completely but, rather, to answer them in a way that allows us to understand the story we find ourselves in - the basics of what God has revealed in the Bible - about himself, about spiritual reality, about mankind, about the reality of evil (where it came from and what it is up to), and about how Christians can live happy, successful, victorious, abundant lives in this sin-sick, cursed world.

ABOUT GOD

What does God tell us about himself in the Bible? The Bible offers no argument for the existence of God. It is simply taken for granted. Theologians have several special words they use to describe God. It is a kind of short-hand to pack a lot of meaning into a few words. The ideas behind each of these words are important because they help us understand what God has told us about Himself. I'll list a few of these words one at a time and then briefly explain what each one means with one or more examples of Bible verses where these ideas can be found. Usually, there are many more verses that could be listed.

- God is self-existent. God exists of or by Himself without the need of any external cause or agency[13].

- God is eternal. God has no beginning and will have no end. He always has been and always will be.[14]

- God is infinite. God is so great that He has no limits and cannot be limited.[15]

- God is self-sufficient. God has the necessary resources and power to do whatever he chooses without help. He is independent.[16]

- God is omnipresent. God is present everywhere and has access to all of reality.[17]

- God is omnipotent. God is all-powerful; almighty.[18]

- God is omniscient. God possesses all knowledge – knows everything - past, present and future.[19]

- God is wise. God always acts with full knowledge and correct values.[20]

- God is immutable. We can always count on God because of His unchanging character and dependability. God doesn't change, either quantitatively or qualitatively. He is what he always has been and always will be.[21]

- God is sovereign. God has supremacy and control over all that occurs.[22]

- God is Holy. God is separate from and above all else - particularly from all evil.[23]

- God is true. God is the ultimate source of truth.[24]

- God is faithful. God always fulfills what he says he will do.[25]

- God is love. God is concerned and takes action for the welfare of his creatures. Many theologians consider love to be the most basic or fundamental of God's attributes.[26]

- God is gracious. God deals with his people not on the basis of what they deserve, but simply in terms of his goodness and generosity relating to their needs.[27]

- God is merciful. God shows compassionate concern for his people and tenderhearted treatment of the needy.[28]

- God is righteous and just. God always acts in a just and fair manner; doing what is right and yet doing what justice demands.[29]

- God is a trinity. The word trinity is a word not found in Scripture, but used to express the specifically Christian doctrine that God is a unity of three distinct Persons; God the Father, God the Son, And God the Holy Spirit. How this could be true is a mystery to the human mind and yet the Bible makes it clear that it is true.[30]

- God is transcendent. He exists outside of the created world and rules over it. He lives in a spiritual world that is separate from the energy, matter, space-time physical world we live in. We are told that:

- God is not alone there, for we read of 'the host of heaven' which worships him[31], and of 'the angels in heaven'[32]. Believers also may look forward to 'an inheritance kept in heaven' for them[33]. Heaven is thus the present abode of God, his angels, and the ultimate destination of his saints on earth.[34]

This list provides us with information on a primarily intellectual basis which is fine as far as it goes. We do need a clear grasp of the intellectual truth about God. To the degree that our mental image of God does not reflect truth about Him, then we can't really know, worship, or relate to Him in 'Spirit and truth' because we are worshiping a 'false' image – in other words, an idol! But, there are also other ways to know

God: experientially and personally. This kind of knowledge of God can only be experienced at a spiritual level. We'll talk more about that kind of knowledge later in this and other chapters.

Now that we have a very basic idea of who God is, it is important to ask the next question: what does He want to accomplish in this world? To answer that question we have to start with the Garden of Eden. God created and placed the first man and woman in a perfect environment (the Garden of Eden). He told them to be fruitful and multiply and increase in number, to fill the earth and subdue it, to rule over the animal world[35], and - not to eat fruit from the Tree of Knowledge of Good and Evil. God told them that, if they did, they would die[36]. Then Satan came along (in the form of the talking snake) and suggested to them that by limiting their access to that tree, God was holding out on them – that, if they ate of it, they would become gods too. Of course, they ate of the fruit from that tree and got thrown out of the garden to keep them from also eating of the Tree of Life and living forever. As a result of their rebellion against God, a curse was placed on them, on the earth[37] and the entire world system came under Satan's control[38]. Unfortunately, we are all experiencing the consequence of their rebellion against God (sin) to this very day.

On the surface, it looks like Satan with Adam's and Eve's cooperation managed to short-circuit what God was trying to do in the Garden of Eden. God's original purpose was for mankind to rule and reign on the earth[39] and we will do it for eternity on the new (re-created) earth. For now, those who know Jesus as their personal savior are still to rule over their own physical and spiritual world in His name, power and authority. The Bible says that those who God knew would accept His free offer of salvation were chosen by God to be adopted into His family. The Bible says this choice was made before the foundations of the world[40]!

So, what happened in the garden was not a surprise to God. You may be wondering why God would allow all of this to happen. Because, our loving, free-will response to His offer of salvation is truly important to Him. The Trinity (Father, Son, and Holy Spirit) have been in a perfect, loving relationship for eternity. He wants as many people as possible to share this relationship with Him for eternity! The Bible tells us that, not only will God's intentions for this earth and his relationship with mankind ultimately will be fulfilled, but, also He has given us a lot of detail about just how it will all happen. Do you want to know more about what God is up to and how this is all going to happen? Keep reading.

ABOUT MANKIND

The Bible says that mankind was created in God's image. This means, in part, that we have been given characteristics that have parallels in God's nature. Kenneth Samples explains:

> Many evangelical theologians comfortably distinguish between *natural image* and the *moral image*. The broader of the two, the natural image, includes constituent aspects of humans' nature – their spiritual, intellectual, volitional, relational, immortal, and powerful capacities. The moral image involves a more restricted sense of God's image based on humans' *original* knowledge, righteousness, and holiness. Adam possessed these qualities in the Garden of Eden before his fall into sin[41].

Samples goes on to say:

> Though human beings were created to reflect God's image, when Adam disobeyed God (Genesis 3) all subsequent humanity inherited sinfulness, guilt, moral corruption, and both physical and spiritual death (Romans 5:12 - 21). In a state of rebellion, all people suffer from a totally depraved nature that keeps them alienated from a holy and just God. This depravity while not making people completely evil, nevertheless corrupts our entire being, including our mind, body, and spirit (Psalms 51:5 58:3; Romans 1:18 - 21; 6:23; 8:7 - 8; Ephesians 2:1 - 3; 4:17 – 19). But to what extent does this condition affect our image of God? Did sin completely erase God's image from mankind? … The moral image necessary for us to have a relationship with God – was eradicated by the fall. Once sin infected humanity, all human beings became unrighteous lawbreakers separated from God (Romans 3:23; Galatians 5:19 – 21). Yet the natural image – though unquestionably tarnished and obscured – was not completely lost. … After the fall, human beings remain God's image bearers (Genesis 9:6; James 3:9), yet in the state of

sin, people are certainly less like God than they were before. …
The total depravity of human beings makes it impossible to live
a God–pleasing life. Consequently, sinful people must depend
on God's saving grace to regenerate a positive relationship with
him and experience salvation[42]

It is hard to know what "die" meant to Adam and Eve when God
told them that they would die if they ate of the fruit - since they probably
had never experienced death. With 20/20 hindsight and the explanation
above, we can now understand that the death that Adam and Eve was
warned about was both physical (they no longer would live forever
physically) and spiritual in the sense that their moral image was lost – i.e.,
their human spirit died - when they sinned and they became separated
from God. Their natural image – i.e., their human soul continued to live
because, when God creates beings who are also given free will (angels
and humans for example), that existence is eternal – either eternal life
or eternal death. Eternal existence is a gift from God we cannot reject;
we can only choose how we will spend it – in total isolation[43] (the Bible
calls this eternal death or hell) or in relationship with others and with
God (the Bible calls this eternal life/heaven). So, the eternal destiny of
creatures like mankind is of infinite importance! At this point in the
story, mankind had been seduced into joining Satan's rebellion against
God. Satan probably thought he had won a great victory. By an act of our
free will, mankind came under Satan's control[44].

Why did God ever allow free will if He knew that it could result in
so much pain and suffering in this world? Many outstanding scholars
and writers have spoken to this subject at length. One brief answer to
these questions has been provided by C.S. Lewis:

> If a thing is to be free to be good, it is also free to be bad.
> And free will is what has made evil possible. Why, then, did
> God give them free will? Because free will, though it makes
> evil possible, is also the only thing that makes possible any love
> or goodness or joy worth having….The happiness which God
> designs for his higher creatures is the happiness of being freely,
> voluntarily united with Him and to each other in an ecstasy
> of love and delight compared with which the most rapturous
> love between a man and a woman on this earth is mere milk

and water. And for that they must be free…. If God thinks this state of war in the universe is a price worth paying for free will – that is, for making a live world in which creatures can do real good or harm and something of real importance can happen, instead of a toy world which only moves when he pulls the strings – then we may take it, it is worth paying.[45]

By the way, God was not caught off guard when all this happened. He had a plan already in place to deal with the mess we got ourselves into. Samples continues:

While the moral image was entirely lost because of the fall, Scripture declares that a saving relationship with Jesus Christ will restore it. The apostle Paul states that through God's grace, believers can "put on the new self, which is being renewed in knowledge in the image of its creator." (Colossians 3:10), be "transformed into his image." (2 Corinthians 3:18), and be "conformed to the image of his son" (Romans 8:29). God the Holy Spirit progressively restores his moral image in the believer through the lifelong process of sanctification (being made righteous in character)[46].

If you are not certain that you have a "saving relationship with Jesus Christ", this is what you need to do right now - recognize the following truths:

- For all have sinned and fall short of the glory of God,[47]

- For the wages of sin is death, but the free gift of God is eternal life in Christ Jesus our Lord.[48]

- For God so loved the world, that He gave His only begotten Son, that whoever believes in Him should not perish, but have eternal life. For God did not send the Son into the world to judge the world, but that the world should be saved through Him. He who believes in Him is not judged; he who does not believe has been judged already, because he has not believed in the name of the only begotten Son of God.[49]

- That's what Christ did definitively: suffered because of others' sins, the Righteous One for the unrighteous ones. He went through it all—was put to death and then made alive—to bring us to God.[50]

- But as many as received Him, to them He gave the right to become children of God, even to those who believe in His name, [51]

At this point, you know enough truth to get this question settled – once and for all. All you need to do is pray this prayer or one like it:

Dear God, I'm not sure that I have a saving relationship with Jesus and I want one. I want to be absolutely sure that I am going to be with you in eternity. I believe that Jesus died for my sins. I accept Jesus as my personal Savior and Lord right now. Thank you for saving me from the consequences of my sins, for adopting me into your family, and for giving your Holy Spirit to live in me. I pray all this in Jesus' name. Amen.

If this is the first time you've prayed a prayer like this, then, *Welcome to the family of God and eternal Life!* Now, I have both some good news and some bad news. Someone has said, "God loves and accepts us into his family just as we are – but He loves us too much to leave us that way". C. S. Lewis puts it this way:

The command *be perfect*[52] is not idealistic gas. Nor is it a command to do the impossible. He is going to make us into creatures that can obey the command. He said (in the Bible) that we were "gods", and He is going to make good His words. If we let Him - for we can prevent him if we choose - He will make the feeblest and filthiest of us into a god or goddess, a dazzling, radiant, immortal creature, pulsating all through with such energy and joy and wisdom and love as we cannot now imagine, a bright stainless mirror which reflects back to God perfectly (though of course on a smaller scale) His own boundless power and delight and goodness. The process will be long and in parts very painful; but it is what we are in for. Nothing less. He meant what he said.[53]

One of the purposes of this book is to explain how we can cooperate with God in the process of becoming more like Jesus and experience all the benefits that come with that process. Jesus said, "The thief (Satan) comes only to steal and kill and destroy; I have come that they may have life, and have it to the full"[54]. I want life to the full! How about you?

ABOUT SATAN

Now, let's focus our attention on the being that was tempting Adam and Eve. Where did he come from? What is he like? What is he up to? Before we get into answering these questions, I want to bring a word of caution. Once we recognize the reality of Satan, and all the deceptions he is up to in our lives, we can become "obsessed with him, fearful of what he's going to do next. Once we take him seriously, he switches from his tactic of "I'm not here" to one of having us worry about him day and night, which is almost a form of worship. …God desires to use the enemy's attacks to remove the obstacles between ourselves and Him, to reestablish our dependency on Him as His sons and daughters in a much deeper way. Once we understand that, the warfare we are in begins to feel totally different."[55] Someone has said that the first rule of warfare is to understand your enemy – so you'll know what tactics to use to defeat him. Satan is a defeated foe[56]. All evil and human sin will be vanquished at Christ's second coming as Judge and Lord[57]. We have no reason to fear him (Satan) when we are living in the authority, power, and position given us in Jesus' name. The power of the Holy Spirit living in us and working through us is far greater than any of the power, schemes, or tactics of Satan[58].

The Bible actually tells quite a lot about Satan. But, first, we need to be reminded again that Satan is not God's equal and opposite (like the idea of Yin/Yang). He is a created being and his power (as great as it may be) when compared to God's infinite power isn't even measureable. He is referred to by several different names. The great dragon, Satan, the adversary, Lucifer, the prince of the power of the air, the devil, our enemy, Beelzebub, the father of lies, the thief, the god of this world, and others. Each of these names tells us, in part, what he is up to. First, though, let's take a look at what the Bible tells us about his history.

Several things are revealed about Satan in the Bible[59] - about what happened in Heaven before tempting Adam and Eve the Garden of Eden and what will happen to him in the end. We're told that Satan was created by God as the model of perfection and perfect in beauty. He was adorned with precious stones and apparently had musical ability. He had a very important place in heaven as the guardian cherub. He was blameless in his ways until the day wickedness was found in him. His heart became proud because of his beauty and he corrupted his wisdom because of his splendor. He led a rebellion against God and intended to establish his throne above God's. He was expelled from heaven along with the angels who followed him and was cast down to earth. Ultimately, Satan and his followers will be thrown into the Lake of Fire where they will stay for eternity.

Much more could be said about Satan's past and his future; but, what is more important for us to know about is what he and his fallen angels, also called evil spirits, or demons, are up to down here on earth until the time of their final judgment. They are making war now against those who have become Christians. John Eldredge puts it this way:

> Until we come to terms with *war* as the context of our days, we will not understand life. We will misinterpret 90% of what is happening around us and to us. It will be very hard to believe that God's intentions toward us are life abundant; it will be even harder not to feel that somehow we are just blowing it. Worse, we will begin to accept some really awful things about God.[60]

We will begin to believe these things because of all the awful things that happen to us and to others all around us in this life here on earth. Eldredge goes on to say:

> Before he promised us life, Jesus warned that the thief would try to steal, kill and destroy it. How come we don't think that the thief then actually steals, kills, and destroys? You won't understand your life, until you see clearly what has happened to you and how to live forward from here, unless you see it as a battle[61]. Being unable to defeat God through raw power, Satan's legions decide to wound God as deeply as possible by stealing the love of his Beloved (us) through seduction. And having "seduced them to his party," to ravish them body and soul; and having ravished them, to mock them even as they are hurled to the depths of hell with God himself unable to save them because of their rejection of him. This is Satan's motivation and goal for every man, woman, and child into whom God ever breathed the breath of life. Like a roaring lion, he "hungers" for us.[62]

The Bible is full of references to and illustrations of the reality of warfare in a Christian's life. For example, Paul tells us to "be strong in the Lord and in His mighty Power. Put on the full armor of God so that you can take your stand against the Devil's schemes. "For our struggle is not against flesh and blood, but against rulers, against the authorities, against the powers of this dark world and against the spiritual forces of evil in the heavenly realms"[63]. Paul then goes on to describe the various pieces of our spiritual armor and tell us to put it on. Charles Haddon Spurgen (1834-1892) served as a preacher and pastor at London's six-thousand seat Metropolitan Tabernacle for thirty years. Spurgen expands further on these ideas:

> War will always rage between the two great sovereignties until one or the other is crushed. Peace between good and evil, is an impossibility; in fact, the very pretense of it would be the triumph of the powers of darkness. *Michael will always fight*[64]; his holy soul is vexed with sin and will not endure it. Jesus will always be the dragon's foe and that not in a quiet sense, but actively, vigorously, with full determination to exterminate evil. All his servants, whether angels in heaven or messengers on earth, will and must fight; they are born to be warriors – at the cross they enter into a covenant never to make a truce with evil; they are a warlike company, firm in defense and fierce in attack. The duty of every soldier in the army of the Lord is daily, with all his heart, and soul, and strength, to fight against the Dragon.[65]

The reason that we find ourselves in a warzone is because we gave up our authority to rule on this earth when we sinned and Satan stepped in to take over. The earth came under his control. Jesus referred to Satan as "the prince of this world"[66]. This could happen only because, when Adam and Eve rebelled against God, they lost their Moral Image of God (in other words, their human spirit died but not their soul) and, with that loss, they lost their God-given authority. Satan could take over simply because there was a power vacuum! But, here is some good news: when we connect with God by accepting Jesus as our savior, the power vacuum in our sphere of influence is filled again with God's power (the Holy Spirit) and God's authority is given to us again[67]. All we have to do as Christians is to choose to use it. We'll learn more about how to do that later.

So, what are Satan and his fallen angels (demons) up to? Satan knows that his time to control the world system is limited and that he has been defeated twice – first, when he and his fallen angels were cast from heaven to earth and the second time, when Jesus paid the price for our sin on the cross and rose from the dead as the ultimate proof of victory over sin and death. He also knows that his third and final defeat will come when he and his demons will be thrown into the lake of fire that has been prepared for him and his fallen angels[68]. Satan is doing everything God will allow him to do to hurt God by hurting all of humankind and trying to convince as many of us as possible to join in his continuing warfare against God. The things that are going on right now in the physical world will convince most people that evil is a reality. The Bible tells us that man's own sin nature and Satan (along with his fallen angels) are the source of that evil. John Eldredge explains it like this:

> Counting on our vanity and blindness, he seduces us to try to control life by living in the smaller stories we all construct to one degree or another. He accuses God to us and us to God. He accuses us through the words of parents and friends and God himself. He calls good evil and evil good and always helps us question whether God has anything good in mind in his plans for us. He steals our innocence as children and replaces it with a blind naïveté or cynicism as adults. At the same time, Satan is at work reinterpreting our individual stories in order to make God our enemy. . . He replaces the love affair with a religious system of do's and don'ts that parch our hearts and replaces our worship and communion with entertainment. Our experience of life deteriorates from the passion of a grand love affair, in the midst of a life–and–death battle, to an endless series of chores and errands, a business that separates us from God, each other, and even from our own thirstiness[69].

Physical vs. Spiritual Realms

The Bible doesn't try to prove that there are both spiritual and physical worlds. Both realms are discussed simply as a matter of factual reality.

For example, when Jesus was being questioned by Pilot just prior to His crucifixion, Pilot asked Him if He was "king of the Jews". Jesus told Pilot in a very matter-of-fact way; "My kingdom is not of this world...."[70] We find another example in what is probably the most quoted verse in the Bible, John 3:16, it says, "God sent His Son into the world...."; implying that Jesus was sent into the world from some other place that is not part of 'this world'. We are told a great deal about what has happened in both realms in the past and what will happen in the future.

Yes, we live in a war zone. We live on a battle field and mankind is the focus of attack and also caught in the crossfire. We have a choice to recognize this reality and become solders on God's side, become a passive victim of all that is happening, or join Satan in his rebellion. If we choose to be a passive victim, we are actually joining Satan's rebellion by rejecting God's free offer of salvation and eternal life[71]. We can decide which choice to make and, by making that choice, we also choose the resulting consequences. When we choose to join God's side, Satan's attacks are focused on us in ways that they were not before. The remainder of this book assumes that you have become a Christian and, as a result are under attack. This is simply the reality we are facing. Ray C. Steadman observes:

> Only the Christian can be led by the Spirit of God into the nature of reality, into truth. Jesus said of the Spirit of truth that the people of this world "cannot accept him, because it neither sees him nor knows him. But you can know him for he lives with you and will be in you." The Spirit of truth is for Christians only. The world will never be able to understand reality! As long as human beings remain worldlings, they are blinded to the ultimate nature of things. They will never understand them because humanity is both the specimen to be examined and the examiner – and the error is that the examiner affects the examination! Human beings reason continually in a vicious circle of unbelief that prevents them from discovering ultimate reality.[72]

The truth is that only Christians have the resources they need, not only to survive the battle, but to be gloriously victorious. What does Satan's attacks look like? What are Satan's strategies? What can we do about it? What are our spiritual resources and weapons? How do we use them? If we've been taken captive (and all of us have at one time or another), how can we get free and rejoin the battle? How can we keep from becoming a captive again?

MIND ATTACK

There is a mighty battle going on for control of your mind.
Heaven and earth intersect in your mind;
the tugs of both spheres influence your thinking.

Sarah Young[1]

"Age and treachery will always defeat youth and zeal." Before we engage
in spiritual warfare, we should know this about Satan:
he is an ancient and extremely treacherous foe.[2]

When we choose to join God's side, Satan's attacks are focused on us in ways that they were not before. What do these attacks look like? What are Satan's strategies? Before we answer these questions, we must first remember that we are beings created in God's image. Although mankind lost part of that image when Adam and Eve joined Satan's rebellion against God, those of us who have received Jesus as our personal savior have not only had the lost part of our Image of God[3] at least partially restored, but, also, have been given the Holy Spirit to live in us as proof that our relationship with God has been re-established[4] and will continue.[5] The Bible says that "If anyone is in Christ, he is a new creation; the old has gone, the new has come!"[6] The Bible also makes it clear that this becoming "a new creation" is a process that progressively restores the full Image of God. The Bible calls this process 'sanctification'. This is a continuing process that ultimately will result in us becoming as much like Jesus as it is possible for created beings to be.[7] But, this process is not for sissies. Charles Swindoll puts it this way:

> God uses an infinite number of vehicles in the process
> of helping us grow. I do not know of any means that leads
> to instant growth. I've never met anyone who became

instantly mature. It's a painstaking process that God takes us through, and includes such things as waiting, failing, losing, and being misunderstood – each one calling for extra doses of perseverance. Christian growth comes through hard–core, gutsy perseverance.[8]

Once we accept that there is a spiritual warfare going on, we may tend to blame Satan for more of our problems than he is actually responsible for. When I write about "Satan" doing this or that, I am really saying that, probably, one of his underlings is doing it. Satan has a well organized army of helpers – the fallen Angels. The Bible says that, "Our struggle is not against flesh and blood, but against the rulers, against the authorities, against the powers of this dark world and against the spiritual forces of evil in the heavenly realms."[9] Language scholars tell us that the various words (such as rulers and authorities) can refer to military rank titles. It might be paraphrased to say that we fight against generals, captains, corporals, and millions of foot soldiers in Satan's army. Also, those involved in spiritual warfare often refer to various evil spirits or demons, by what those spirits are trying to accomplish in our lives like fear, anger, unforgiveness, addiction, etc. For example, we might call a demon the spirit of fear or the spirit of anger.

Satan can never keep us from ultimately receiving all that God has promised us. What he can do though is to try to get us to believe things that are not true. In the Garden of Eden, Satan said, "Did God *really* say …? You shall *not* surely die"; tempting Eve to question what God had really said and then telling her an outright lie. He wants to do anything he can to limit God's work in our lives. If we believe his lies, it sets us up to fall prey to his temptation so he can get us into bondage. Satan wants us to focus on anything else but the truth that people are separated from God and that, nevertheless, we are unconditionally loved by God and invited to become His sons and daughters by accepting His free gift of salvation. Jesus said, "I am the way and the truth and the life. No one comes to the father except through me.[10]" He also said, "If you hold to my teaching, you are really my disciples. Then you will know the truth and the truth will set you free.[11]" So, experiencing Truth (Jesus) and truth (from the Bible) is the key to staying free. Charles Swindoll wrote:

Want a challenge? Start modeling the truth...the whole truth and nothing but the truth, so help you God. Think truth. Confess truth. Face truth. Love truth. Pursue truth. Walk truth. Talk truth. Ah, that last one! That's a good place to begin. From this day forward, deliberately, consciously, and conscientiously speak the truth. Start practicing gut–level authenticity....[12]

So, just what is the truth? In the last chapter, we discussed a way of seeing reality that exposed us to a lot of truth. The truth we were exposed to was part of seeing the big picture. To use the thousand-piece puzzle illustration, we received a general description of what the puzzle actually looks like so we can begin to put it together. The real question, at this point, is what do we do with the pieces of the puzzle that are part of our individual, day-to-day lives? Understanding the big picture gives us a good place to begin to understand what is going on in our own lives. Reading the Bible (especially the New Testament) will help us understand even more of the "Truth". The word truth is capitalized in the last sentence because it includes understanding more about Jesus (God's living Word) and what He taught, as well as, His written Word – what the early church understood and believed about God and how He wants to relate to us as individuals.

What we choose to do and how we choose to do it in our individual lives depends on what we believe to be true. If we believe that there is no way that we can know real truth, that all "truth" is relative, that this physical world is all there is to reality, then we will live our life based on what we think is true. If, on the other hand, we have become a Christian by accepting Jesus as our personal savior, and we understand that there is much more to reality than what our senses or scientific instruments can reveal to us, then we will live and behave in ways very different from those who don't believe these things. The problem we all face is that we are bombarded every day with information designed to influence what we believe is true. Just think about how many commercials we see or hear every day. Think about the information we are confronted with on TV, radio, in printed news or in books. From our earliest years as children we are influenced by our parents, our friends, our relatives, our teachers, our coaches, our pastors, our culture, our history – the list is almost endless. As mature adults, most of us have developed some defensive or evaluative coping skills; but, as children, teenagers, and young adults, and sometimes, as adults, we are rarely fully equipped to process all that comes at us accurately or completely. Much of this information may have been intended to be helpful. A lot of it, however, was inappropriate for our level of maturity or knowledge, outright misleading, manipulative, simply not true, and intentionally (or unintentionally) hurtful or painful to us. As a result, we are potentially hurt or damaged by the things we experience in our normal, everyday lives. Karl Lehman, M.D., a Christian psychiatrist, has observed:

> When we encounter pain, our brain–mind–spirit always tries to process the painful experience. There is a very deliberate pathway that this pain processing attempt will follow, and there are specific processing tasks that we must complete as we travel along this pathway, such as maintaining an organized attachment, staying connected, staying relational, navigating the situation in a satisfying way, and correctly interpreting the meaning of the experience. When we are able to successfully complete this processing journey, we get through the painful experience, without being traumatized – we emotionally and cognitively "metabolize", the experience in a healthy way, and instead of having any traumatic power in our lives, the adequately processed painful experience contributes to our knowledge, skills, empathy, wisdom, and maturity. That is, when we successfully process a painful experience, we don't just stuff it down into our unconscious, or teach ourselves to think about other things. We actually get through it, stronger and wiser. There is an old saying, "Suffering will either make you bitter or better." Successfully completing the pain processing pathway is what ensures that we get "better", rather than "bitter."[13]

Dr. Lehman goes on to describe what happens when we don't successfully complete the pain processing process:

> Unfortunately, various problems and/or limitations can block successful processing; and when we are *not* able to complete the processing journey, then the painful experience becomes a traumatic experience and the memories for these traumatic experiences carry unresolved traumatic content....

this unresolved toxic content has lots of negative effects, ...
you don't need the overwhelming negative emotions and
physical pain of military combat or tsunami disasters to create
psychological trauma. In fact, if you are a child, [you need
someone] who can help make sure you get through the pain
processing pathway successfully. ... the painful experience
presents a challenge where your personal processing skills are
especially weak, ...even psychological trauma, especially from
minor painful events, is much more common than most people
realize, and...nobody is completely free of memories carrying
unresolved traumatic content.[14]

So, let's look at what we know so far. Satan tries to get us to focus
on anything but the truth and tries to get us to believe his lies whenever
possible. We live in a world and culture that tries to influence us to
believe things that are often not true. Virtually all of us have memories
and experiences that have been hurtful to us and have not been processed
completely resulting in memories with traumatic content. By the way,
not all lies are completely false. C. S. Lewis has observed that all *powerful*
lies are based on a truth.[15] Someone else has said that the most believable
lies are the ones with the greatest percentage of truth.

Stay with me now – this gets a little technical but it will really be worth
the understanding we'll get from it. Dr. Lehman explains that information
gets stored in our memories in two very different ways. One way is in
our "normal, 'conscious' memory (he calls it our explicit memory). These
memories feel subjectively to us like, "we are remembering something
from our personal past experience". The second way we remember things
is in what Dr. Lehman calls our 'implicit' memory. This kind of memory
does not "feel" like what we think of as memory, because, we do not have
any awareness that we are remembering or that we are being affected
by past experience. Implicit memory is very helpful and important to
us because it is where we store the knowledge of how to do things that
we rarely need to think about like walking, or feeding ourselves, or
driving our car. Implicit memory is sometimes referred to as "invisible"
memory, since it usually affects us without being "seen" by our conscious
minds. There is a lot of rigorous, medical, scientific evidence proving the
existence of implicit memory as separate from explicit memory. Now,
here is the part that helps us understand why memories with traumatic

content (memories of experiences that have hurt us and have led us to believe things that are not true) can get us in such trouble; they are stored in our implicit, 'invisible' memory.[16]

> When something in the present triggers a traumatic memory, the unresolved content from the trauma, such as the distorted beliefs and emotions associated with the original painful experience, will come forward as "invisible" implicit memory **that feels true and valid in the present**. (Dr. Lehman's emphasis)[17]

We have another marvelous ability built into our brain. It helps us explain, organize, and make sense out of our experiences and the world around us. Dr. Lehman calls this our Verbal Logical Explainer (VLE). The VLE works so quickly and smoothly that we don't even realize what it is doing. At this very moment, it is working to help you make sense out of your experience as you read this book.[18]

> Our VLE's ... usually start with basic adequate and accurate data, and come up with basically valid explanations. However, if our VLE's start with distorted and/or inadequate data, we can come up with profoundly flawed explanations. For example, if my VLE starts with thoughts and emotions that are from....an invisible implicit memory *so that they feel true in the present and I have no awareness of their original origin,* my VLE will make up explanations for how these thoughts and emotions are being caused by circumstances in the present....[19]

Why are we so open to believing things that may not be true? We are being influenced by lies and hurts from a wide range of experiences and sources without even realizing what it is happening to us! We have two more things going on in our "brain-mind-spirit" system. The first of these tricks our mind plays on us is what Dr. Lehman calls "Confabulation":

> Confabulation is a special kind of fabrication in which the person makes something up based on their best guess regarding what might be the answer, but with *no conscious awareness that they are guessing and with no deliberate intent to deceive*....We all engage in much more subtle forms of confabulation when our VLEs are unknowingly working with raw material that includes "invisible" implicit memory content....and (we) appear to be

completely unaware of the fact that his VLE has just given an explanation that is only a wild guess – a guess that actually has *nothing* to do with the real reason for [our] actions. Children have Verbal Logical Explainer's that are still quite primitive, and therefore provide yet another place where it's easy to recognize that the VLE often makes things up.[20]

The second of these tricks our mind plays on us is something we have all experienced – often without recognizing that it is happening. This is our amazing and very human capacity for denial and self-deception. Finally, Dr. Lehman observes:

I think the last pieces of the puzzle are good old denial and self-deception. Most of us don't want to know just how dysfunctional we really are: we don't want to see how often we are triggered; we don't want to see just how many of our perceptions, thoughts, and emotions are implicit memories coming from unresolved trauma; and we don't want to see how many of our explanations are actually VLE confabulations trying to justify our triggered reactions. So we look away from the clues that tell us that something's missing. We look away from the evidence telling us "Something's wrong with this picture." We look away from the data points that tell us something's wrong with the way we understand ourselves and the world around us. We look away from the evidence pointing to the flaws in our VLE confabulated explanations.... It's pretty easy to maintain a blind spot when we don't want to see what's hiding in the blind spot and when we don't want to know we have a blind spot. To put this another way: it's amazing how easy it is to be fooled when were fooling ourselves and we want to be fooled.[21]

Now that we understand a lot more about how our brain-mind-spirit system works and why it is so easy for us to fool ourselves, let's take a look at what others have had to say about what is happening to us.

C. S. Lewis wrote, "For there are two things inside of me, competing with the human self which I must try to become. They are the Animal self, and the Diabolical self. The Diabolical self is the worst of the two."[22] The "animal" self is the source of our appetites for self-gratification. Most of these are not, in themselves, a source of temptation to do things that are morally or ethically wrong. They are the natural desires and needs of our physical brain and body. Our "diabolical" self (i.e. our sin nature), on the other hand, will take our natural desires or needs and use them to tempt us to do or think, or believe things that *are* wrong. This "wrong" can be as subtle as overeating or over-doing anything that we desire or think we need.

The Bible says that there are three primary sources of temptation: the world, the flesh, and the devil.[23] Our diabolical self is what the Bible calls our *flesh*. The "world" includes several other sources of temptation. First there are other's "selves" – both their "flesh" and their sin-natures – that can draw us away from what we know is right and into what we may or may not recognize is wrong. These temptations can be very subtle or very obvious. Others can also be used either consciously or unconsciously by Satan to create, or make use of, potentially traumatic experiences that can lead us into all kinds of trouble without us even realizing what is happening. The "world" also includes the full array of cultural influences that can lead us into seeing things in ways that will result in our intentionally or unintentionally doing things that are wrong. Remember also that Satan is called "the god of this world"[24] and he is temporarily in control of the world's political and cultural systems. You can be sure that he and his demonic helpers are doing everything they can to indoctrinate us into seeing things from their perspective and joining their rebellion against God. One reason he can be so successful is because, "…due to his great age and dark wisdom, Satan knows us better than we know ourselves. The one purpose of his heart is the destruction of all that God loves, particularly his beloved [us]. He stalks us day and night, as the Lord tells us through Peter: "Your enemy the devil prowls around like a roaring lion looking for someone to devour" (1 Peter 5:8)."[25]

This sounds like a lot of focus on Satan and his helpers; but only so that we can "be aware of his schemes.[26]" John Eldredge puts it this way:

> Finally, he probes the perimeter, looking for weaknesses. Here's how this works: Satan will throw a thought or a temptation at us in hopes that we will swallow it…. When Satan probes, make no agreements. If we make an agreement, if something in our heart says *yeah, you're right*, then, he pours it

on. You'll see a beautiful woman and something inside you will say you want her. That's the evil one appealing to the traitor within. If the traitor says *yes I do*, then, the lust really begins to take hold. Let that go on for years, and you have given him a stronghold. This can make a good man feel so awful because he thinks he's a lustful man when he's not; it's an attack through and through . Please don't misunderstand me. I'm not blaming everything on the devil. In almost every situation, there are human issues involved. Every man has his struggles; every marriage has its rough spots; every ministry has personal conflicts. But those issues are like a campfire that the Enemy throws gasoline all over and turns into a bonfire. The flames leap up into a raging inferno and we are suddenly overwhelmed with what we're feeling. Simple misunderstandings become grounds for divorce. All the while we believe that it's us, we are blowing it, were to blame, and the enemy is laughing because we've swallowed the lie "I'm not here, it's just you." We've got to be a lot more cunning than that.[27]

I want to introduce you now to two words that we will explore in greater detail in later chapters: "strongholds" and "footholds". These words sound similar but they represent two very different and important areas of truth. First we'll look at strongholds. The Bible says:

> For, though we live in the world, we do not wage war as the world does. The weapons we fight with are not the weapons of the world. On the contrary, they have divine power to demolish strongholds. We demolish arguments and every pretension that sets itself up against the knowledge of God, and we take captive every thought to make it obedient to Christ. [28]

The spiritual weapons available to us to "demolish strongholds" will be discussed in the next chapter –Resources. The key issue for now is that we are expected to use spiritual power to demolish strongholds. So, what are strongholds? When we look up the word in the original language (*ochuroma*), we are told that its meaning includes: "1. a castle, stronghold, a fortress ....2. anything on which one relies....2a. arguments and reasoning by which a disputant endeavors to fortify his opinion and defend it...."[29] The Bible text itself tells us which definition we are to use: "….We demolish arguments and every pretension that sets itself up against the *knowledge* of God…." The strongholds the Bible tells us we are supposed to pull down are beliefs or belief systems that have been set up in our brain or mind that does not represent truth or reality. Another way of saying this is that a stronghold is any lie or deception that we have intentionally or unintentionally chosen to believe. The Bible doesn't use the word 'stronghold' in this way often. But, it does have a great deal to say about its synonyms: deceptions and lies. John Eldredge simply says we "make an agreement with" lies. The *Restoring the Foundations* ministry refers to these deceptions or lies as "Ungodly Beliefs". Dr. Lehman refers to them in a more psychologically thorough way as "memories or thoughts with 'traumatic' content, VLE confabulations, denial, and self-deception". By whatever name you call them, strongholds inhibit effective brain functioning, evaluation of thoughts, and decision making about appropriate behaviors.

To me, the most insidious thing about strongholds is that they usually operate without our realizing that we are being affected by them. In other words, they are in a "blind-spot" of our awareness and set us up to be "blind-sided" by the world, the flesh, or the Devil! How can we keep this from happening? How can we recognize strongholds? Once we have recognized them, what can we do to get rid of them? We will answer these questions and many others in later chapters about strongholds.

When we behave in ways that are based on the desires of our sinful nature and not based on truth and reality, our behaviors will be, at the best, inappropriate and, at the worst, what the Bible calls 'sinful'. What is so bad about acting in sinful ways? Because, acting in sinful ways have *horrible* consequences. Sin results in:

Separation from God[30]

God's face being hidden from us[31]

Keeping God from hearing our prayers[32]

Us not measuring up to God's standard[33]

Keeping us from pleasing God[34]

Ending up in slavery to sin[35]

Ending up in captivity to the 'law of sin'[36]

The Bible also says that when we sin, we give the Devil a "foothold".[37] The word "foothold" in the original language (*topos*) means "...a place, any portion or space marked off, as it were from surrounding space.... an inhabited place, as a city, village...."[38] Jesus said, "I go to prepare a place for you...."[39] This is the same word used in "don't give the devil a "place". When we sin, we give Satan a "place" of influence in our life related to that particular sin. The more we sin in that area, the greater that influence becomes. This does not mean that we (as Christians) are, in any way, indwelt or controlled by Satan. I want to make this very clear – those who are truly Christians can never be indwelt by Satan because we are already indwelt by the Holy Spirit. The Bible says that the Holy Spirit is greater (infinitely more powerful) than Satan.[40] But, that doesn't mean that he can't try to influence us to sin so that, when we do (and ultimately, we all do), he can get an area of influence in our lives and bring us into bondage to his influence. We are all aware of how much easier it is to sin in a particular way once we have begun to sin repeatedly in that area. It becomes like a habit, a compulsion, or an addiction. Even the apostle Paul (someone most of us think of as a 'super-Christian') knew what this was like:

> I do not understand what I do. For what I want to do I do not do, but what I hate I do.... I have the desire to do what is good, but I cannot carry it out. For what I do is not the good I want to do; no, the evil I do not want to do — this I keep on doing.... So I find this law at work: When I want to do good, evil is right there with me. For in my inner being I delight in God's law; but I see another law at work in the members of my body, waging war against the law of my mind and making me a prisoner of the law of sin at work within my members. What a wretched man I am! Who will rescue me from this body of death? Thanks be to God—through Jesus Christ our Lord! So then, I myself in my mind am a slave to God's law, but in the sinful nature a slave to the law of sin.[41]

Yes, we all experience what Paul was describing. But, Christians are not left as hopeless slaves to sin. Paul then goes on to say:

> Therefore, there is now no condemnation for those who are in Christ Jesus, because through Christ Jesus the law of the

Spirit of life set me free from the law of sin and death. For what the law was powerless to do in that it was weakened by the sinful nature, God did by sending his own Son in the likeness of sinful man to be a sin offering. And so he condemned sin in sinful man, in order that the righteous requirements of the law might be fully met in us, who do not live according to the sinful nature but according to the Spirit.[42]

So, to summarize, we all end up with satanic footholds in our lives. This means that Satan can use these special areas of satanic influence in our lives to keep us sinning (if we let him) so we will continue to experience the terrible consequences of sin in our lives. If we are truly Christians, he can't sever our *relationship* with God. But, he can disrupt our *fellowship* with God - because of the consequences of sin. What can we do to get rid of these footholds? Can we keep them from being re-established in our lives? We will answer these questions and many others in a later chapter about footholds.

I have been a pastor and counselor for almost forty years. A pastoral counselor's primary job is to help people learn how to apply Biblical truth in their lives – not to deal with mental illness, although, mental illness may be cured or significantly helped as people apply the truth of God's word in their lives. In my opinion, pastoral counselors should always collaborate with licensed, Christian mental health professionals whenever mental illness seems to be an issue. This would, of course, include the use of prescribed medication when appropriate.

In my earlier years of ministry, I did my best to help those who came to me to apply Biblical truth in their lives – nearly always with some success. About twenty years ago, I was introduced to concepts about 'footholds' though Cleansing Stream Ministries.[43] As I started to use these concepts in my pastoral counseling ministry, I was thrilled to see people freed from what seemed to be compulsive impulses to continue in the sinful behaviors that they had come for help with. As time went by, however, many of the same people came back again for help in dealing with the same problems they had been clearly freed from several weeks or months earlier. What was causing them to get back into bondage to demonic influence again? Was it habit? Was it lack of discipline? Was it lack of willpower? Was it lack of faith? As I worked further with them, I began to realize that these people were harboring beliefs about themselves, about others, and about God that were rooted in difficult, hurtful and, sometimes, very painful experiences in their lives. Many of these experiences happened early in their lives (things like emotional or verbal abuse, physical abuse, sexual abuse, rape, frightening situations, and many others). As a result, they began to believe things that, even a casual observer, could see were not true. They believed things like: "I've messed up so badly that God could never love me". "I'm beyond hope". "I'm just stupid." "I'm dirty" "I'm ugly". "I'm not worth bothering with". "My feelings don't count". "I don't belong". "If something is wrong, it is my fault". "I'm a bad person". "My only value is in what I do". "I have to keep proving myself". "All love is conditional". "I will always be _____ (afraid, insecure, shy, jealous, angry, easily hurt, taken advantage of, etc.)". "I'll never measure up". "I'll never be _____ (happy, safe, content, appreciated, married, valued for who I am, etc.)".... This list could go on for pages. These are typical strongholds that can lead us into temptation and result in sinful behaviors that then result in a footholds being established or, in the case of those I was working with, re-established. Unless we replace the lies (strongholds) with truth, we will almost certainly end up caught again and again in one foothold after another. I had been helping people get rid of their footholds but I had not been helping them recognize and deal with their strongholds. They were caught in a vicious cycle! No wonder they kept coming back every few months feeling guilty, ashamed, hopeless, angry at themselves, and feeling confused. Here is the good news: Once a stronghold has been recognized and replaced with the truth and the related footholds have been removed, we can have long-term, continuing victory over sinful behaviors that have plagued us our whole lives. Is it possible to re-establish a stronghold? Yes, but, we don't have to. We'll discuss more about how to avoid doing that in later chapters. The important truth is that we can live our lives in freedom from the bondage to our sin nature and Satan. And, we can experience the "...eternal life, more and better life than we ever dreamed of..."[44] the kind of life that Jesus came to give us.

Not only have I seen this process repeated many dozens of times in the lives of those I have counseled, I have personally experienced this same vicious cycle over and over again until I began recognizing the strongholds in my own life. I'll share just one example from my own experience for now.

I was born in 1935. I was raised in a Christian, middle-class family – one father, one mother, and one younger brother. I received Jesus as my Savior at the age of 12 but not as the Lord of my life till much later. My parents wanted to encourage me to succeed at various endeavors so they began offering me "rewards" (praise, a treat, money, etc.) for achievement from an early age. Although it may not have been true, at the time, it seemed to me that they loved and approved of me only when I over-achieved. With school grades, for example, I got a dollar for each "A", a quarter for a "B", and nothing for a "C" or lower. By the time I reached my adult years, one particular set of related strongholds that I had made agreements with included lies like: "All love is conditional", "If I want to be loved and accepted, I have to over-achieve", "Because I'll never completely measure up, I'll never really be loved or accepted", "I'll never really be 'good enough'", "I'm not worth loving", "I have to earn respect, acceptance, and love", "I will never be loved and accepted for who I am", "If I am ever really 'known', I will be rejected", and, "I always have to be useful, capable, highly productive, knowledgeable, and 'do it right'". This was a whole 'nest' of inter-related lies.

If I had not been gifted by God with a wide range of abilities, I probably would have rebelled against all the pressure to achieve and gone the other way. But for the grace of God, I could well have ended up on the scrap-heap of human failure; addicted, criminal, rejected, homeless, and in a downward spiral to who-knows-where. Instead, I took the socially acceptable way - overachievement - doing all the 'right' things but for all the wrong reasons. By the way, when given a choice of how to behave when confronted with this kind of a situation, a person will almost always choose one of these two extremes. They will either move toward self-hatred, with its related self-destructive behaviors, or move toward whatever is opposite of the lies and try to prove that they are not true – even though, subconsciously (in their implicit memory), they really believe that the lies are true. Either extreme results godless, sinful behavior. Either behavioral extreme is focused on 'self' and leads to demonic bondage. In my case, I became an Eagle Scout, graduated from high school with straight 'A's, went to college, had a successful career in management in the aerospace industry, earned an MBA, and, after I became a pastor, I went back to school and earned a Doctor of Ministry degree, and later a Ph.D. in Theology (again with straight 'A's). The Bible says that if I do (all kinds of wonderful things) and don't have 'Love', I am *nothing* … and I gain *nothing*.[45] At the time all this was happening, I didn't have a clue about all the lies (strongholds) I had chosen to make agreements with. They were all in a 'blind-spot' as far as my conscious mind was concerned. If someone would have confronted me with the set of strongholds I listed above, I would have denied them all and told them that they were crazy because, I was 'happy' and 'successful'. I won't list all the footholds these lies led me into, but there were many.

The process of recognizing and replacing strongholds with truth and getting rid of footholds is a bitter-sweet experience. Bitter to recognize the rottenness that has masqueraded as truth in our minds for so long and the sweetness and joy of discovering the real truth that will set us free in so many areas of our lives.

RESOURCES

As Christians, we are superbly equipped both to live the
Christian life and to do battle with evil in Jesus' name.

-DGS-

All Scripture is God-breathed and is useful for teaching, rebuking,
correcting, and training in righteousness, so that the man of God may
be thoroughly equipped [given the resources needed] for every good work.[1]

At this point in our journey together, I hope that you are fully motivated to get rid of the garbage that has accumulated in your life. Believe me, when I learned the things you have just been exposed to, I was motivated too. Now, I have both good news and bad news for you. The good news is that, if you are a Christian, you already have all the resources you need. You may not know right now what they are or how to use them – but you *do* have them available to you. The bad news is that, if you are not a Christian yet, you don't have the spiritual resources that you'll need to get free from bondage. If you are not sure you are a Christian, go back and reread chapter one, accept Jesus as your personal Savior and Lord - then return to this chapter. If you don't do that, you're wasting your time to read any further.

How many of you have watched *Star Wars* and thought: "I wish I could be a Jedi Knight, defending the innocent and battling evil in heroic confrontations"? How many of you have watched the *Lord of the Rings*, and thought, "I wish I could stand beside Aragorn, fighting the forces of darkness in a heroic and righteous quest"? Well, I haven't seen any death stars, orcs, or trolls lately, but our true enemy makes the *Star Wars* emperor and Middle Earth's Sauron look like my grandmother, and Jesus – *our* commander who is *always* standing beside us – makes Aragorn look like a Cub Scout (a good Cub Scout and heroic Cub Scout, but a Cub Scout nonetheless). We have our opportunities if we choose to accept them....[2]

God has given us all the resources we will need to deal with the battles we experience in our lives. The Bible tells us, "His divine power has given us everything we need for life and godliness through our knowledge of him who called us by his own glory and goodness."[3] We *do* have *real life* opportunities to battle the forces of evil. The outcome of these battles will have eternal consequences for us and for others either for good or for evil. As we start to consider the resources we have available to us, we need to recognize, first and foremost, that these are *spiritual* weapons God has given us to use *in His power*. The moment we start to think that we are somehow using our *own power* to do battle – to fight evil in the heavenly (or earthly) places in our own power – we are in big trouble and Satan or any one of his helpers will easily wipe up the floor with us. Remember, Jesus said that without Him we could do nothing.[4] If you need to read this paragraph again to get it indelibly imprinted in your memory, do it! The Bible says that God's strength and power show themselves most effectively in our weakness.[5]

The Bible also says, "Submit yourselves, then, to God. Resist the devil, and he will flee from you."[6] The first prerequisite, if we are going to make the devil flee, is to 'submit ourselves to God (and, by extension, to the leadership He has established – both secular and spiritual leadership)'. What does this mean? When we recognize that the resources we use are *delegated* to us by God for use *only in His power* and, when we choose to use these resources only in this way, then, we are truly 'submitting ourselves to God'. The spiritual power we have in us is God's power.[7] The second prerequisite is to 'resist (stand firm against[8]) the devil'. We can be *absolutely assured* that refusing to cooperate with Satan's temptations by using the resources we are given to resist him will result in his having to flee from us (i.e. from God's power working through us). It is a stimulating, almost giddy, thing to experience this happening – so, don't forget whose power is doing it. Remember, Satan's fall was caused by pride. We need to be sure we don't get caught in the same trap.

These resources are presented in the context of spiritual warfare because that is what this book is primarily about. However, as you learn more about each resource, you will quickly discover that their use is much broader than only their use in spiritual warfare. These are also many of the resources that will allow you to live a successful, victorious, joy-filled, Christian life even when you find yourself in a situation (however rare that might be) that involves no obvious spiritual warfare.

Although these resources are listed individually, they all interact and overlap. For instance, many of the promises of the Bible involve prayer and much of our prayer is based on the promises in God's Word, the Bible. For example, we are told that we are to eat our food gladly with thankful hearts because we know it is made holy by the Word of God and by prayer.[9]

With these cautions in mind, let's take a look at the resources we have been given:

Authority – Jesus gave us the authority to overcome all the power of the enemy[10]. *The Greek word used is "exousia".* It means the rightful, actual, and unimpeded power to act, or to possess, control, or use something. It signifies power that is in some sense lawful. It can be used with the stress on either the rightfulness of power really held, or the reality of power rightfully possessed…[11] Jesus had all authority given him by his Father[12] and He delegated it to us. We will have to answer for the way we use it. Using Jesus' name *is* using the authority he gave us. When we use Jesus' name, we have absolute authority over Satan and his forces! Just be sure you "…use your spiritual authority administratively, compassionately, but never presumptuously. …be bold but never brash or arrogant as you war against the enemy."[13]

Power –The apostle Paul writes that wants us to know about "…the incredibly great power we have been given…."[14]. The Greek word he used was *"dynamis"*. This word means physical power, ability, or strength[15]. Our English word 'dynamite' has this word as its root. This is the same used to describe the Holy Spirit's power that raised Jesus from the dead and seated him at God's right hand.[16] So, we have the irresistible, absolute power of God the Holy Spirit living within us to use in Jesus' name to fight Satan and his forces.

Position – The Bible also says that we are seated *in Jesus* in heavenly places at God's right hand[17]. This is *the* place of honor - far above all earthly or demonic authority, power, and dominion and every title that can be given![18] There is no higher position that a human can occupy than the one we have been given in Jesus.

Just these three resources alone would guarantee that, when we give commands to the enemy in Jesus' name, the enemy has no choice but to obey. Do we have other resources? You Bet! The following is just a partial list.

Spiritual Armor – Paul opens his discussion of our spiritual armor by reminding us what we are up against: "…the spiritual forces of evil in heavenly realms…". Paul continues his discussion of our warfare by listing several pieces of "armor" we are to put on. Just as each piece of armor supports and is inter-related with other pieces of armor, in the same way our spiritual armor is interrelated with each of the others. If Jesus has won the victory, why do we need to put on armor and be involved in warfare? Because, Satan's ultimate and final defeat (when he and his fallen angels are thrown into the lake of fire) is still in the future. Satan knows his time is short (as measured on an eternal time-scale) and that he has no hope of victory. So, he simply wants to cause as much pain and heartache to God and the objects of God's love (humankind) as he can in whatever time he has left. The "armor" that we are given to put on are some of the gifts of Grace we get from God. These are the characteristics that God is building into the lives of every Christian as we cooperate with Him. The purpose of "putting on" these characteristics is so we can "stand against the devil's schemes"[18]. We are told to "be strong in the Lord and in His mighty power[19]. "This command is best understood as a 'passive' command, meaning 'be made strong, be strengthened'…and indicates that believers do not empower themselves …"[20]. Notice, by the way, that there is no armor for our back side. We are to resist not run from the attacks of the devil. "The best thing you can do is turn, face the attack, and deal with it. Now.[21] The armor listed is:[22]

Belt of Truth – This truth is the truth of God's Word; the knowledge of who we are in Jesus; our delegated authority, power, and position in Him; our protection as we enter into spiritual warfare (the armor we are discussing and the promises that we are given in the Bible – like, "nothing will hurt us" Luke 10:19); our spiritual gifts and the fruit of the spirit (discussed below); the promise that Jesus will never leave us or forsake us [23]; the list could fill libraries full of books on this subject alone. Someone has said that 'knowledge is power'. It is also protection.

Breastplate of Righteousness – This is our right-standing and reconciliation with God through all that Jesus accomplished for us. This is God's own righteousness.

Gospel of Peace (covering our feet) – includes not only "good news" of peace with God through Jesus but also peace with each other. – allowing us to function in unity and mutual love with people who are very different from ourselves because we share the same Father, Savior, and the Holy Spirit living within us.[24] This peace with each other includes the mutual support of other believers also engaging in warfare with us, using the same spiritual weapons we are using.

Shield of Faith – The Bible defines faith as, "...FAITH is the assurance (the confirmation, the title deed) of the things [we] hope for, being the proof of things [we] do not see *and* the conviction of their reality [faith perceiving as real fact what is not revealed to the senses]."[25] When we accept the truth of the Bible in faith, we tap into a quality, a level of reality available to us in no other way. The shield referred to here is not the small round shield which left most of the body unprotected, but the large rectangular shield carried by Roman soldiers, which covered the whole person. This shield was substantial and had hooks on the edges so a soldier could connect his shield with those fighting next to him, making a nearly impenetrable shell all around and above the group of inter-connected soldiers - as long as each one stood firm or they moved cooperatively together as a unit. We too can hook our shields of faith together as we support and strengthen each other. Our shield of faith is a gift of God's grace. The Bible says, "For it is by grace you have been saved, through faith - and this not from yourselves, it is the gift of God - not by works, so that no one can boast. For we are God's workmanship, created in Christ Jesus to do good works, which God prepared in advance for us to do."[26]

Helmet of Salvation – A helmet protects the head and the brain/mind within it. Our salvation guarantees the potential availability of all the resources we are discussing in this chapter. This includes not only the resources needed to wage spiritual warfare, but also, God's power working within us to give us the ability to live the 'life abundant' Jesus said he came to bring us; a victorious, power-filled, joy-filled life. There are things we can do or allow in our lives that will limit the full availability of these resources in our lives. We will discuss these things later in this chapter.

Sword of the Spirit (the Word of God) – We are told directly that the sword of the Spirit is the Word of God. This weapon allows us to go on the offensive against the powers of darkness. The term used refers to the short-handled, double-edged sword, which was an important offensive weapon used in close combat. The expression 'the sword of the Spirit'… indicates that the (Holy) Spirit makes the sword powerful and effective, giving to it its cutting edge – 'able to divide soul and spirit, joints and marrow, and judge the thoughts and attitudes of the heart.'[27] This sword of the Spirit is identified with the "word of God', a term which Paul often uses to signify the Gospel. However, he normally uses the Greek word *logos* ('word') instead of Greek word *rhema (pronounced 'ree-mah'),* which appears here.[28] The use of the word '*rhema*' is significant because it indicates a special 'word' (or revelation) from God. In this case the 'word' is given to be used in spiritual warfare. Often, this 'word from God' will be in the form of guidance to use a particular verse or group of verses or a specific truth from the Bible that applies to the situation you are dealing with. We'll say more about the use of this word '*rhema*' as we discuss God's promises to us later in this chapter.

Prayer – Although not specifically identified as a piece of armor, prayer can be an offensive as well as a defensive weapon.

Spiritual Gifts - In the broad sense, the concept of "…spiritual gifts includes a variety of free gifts given by God ranging from spiritual salvation (Rom. 6:23) and temporal rescue (2 Cor. 1:11) to celibacy and marriage (1 Cor. 7:7). In the special or technical usage, spiritual gifts are the particular endowments given by the Spirit to all believers that enable them to serve others for the building up of the church (cf. 1 Co 12:4–7; 1 Peter 4:10). Paul emphasizes the diversity [of spiritual Gifts] that is to be found in the church, the body of Christ, as reflected in the various spiritual gifts (1 Cor. 12:1–31; Rom. 12:3–8). Indeed, the variety of types of gifts is remarkable. Scholars have made various attempts to classify the types of gifts…"28 One such classification (James D. G. Dunn) makes these distinctions:

(1) Activities (miracles, healing, faith)

(2) Manifestations (revelation of Christ, vision and ecstasy, knowledge and wisdom, guidance)

(3) Inspired utterance (proclamation, prophecy, discerning of spirits, teaching, singing, prayer, tongues, interpretation)

(4) Service (giving and caring, helping and guiding).[29]

Some church traditions teach that spiritual gifts were available for Christians to use only early in the history of the church (prior to the completion of the Bible as we have it today). A study of the church throughout church history, however, will reveal that spiritual gifts have been experienced by Christians throughout history and all around the world. I think the reports of these occurrences in the United States are less frequent today because many Christians have not been taught to expect them in our 'scientific, rational age'. It has been my consistent observation that, even in church traditions where spiritual gifts are not expected, they happen all the time. They are just described in a different way. Words of Wisdom might be described as an intuition, an impression, a hunch, just something that occurred to me or, just a thought that popped into my awareness; and, doctors sometimes refer to healing miracles as 'spontaneous remissions'. These are just a few examples.

Spiritual gifts are given to individual believers by the Holy Spirit when they accept Jesus as their Savior and Lord. Each Christian receives only those spiritual gifts that God wants him or her to use to help other Christians at a specific point in time. Spiritual gifts are given to us as seeds that must be developed. As we get rid of strongholds and footholds in our lives, we are getting free of bondages of the enemy and are being built up to progressively become more and more like Jesus. So, in that sense, spiritual gifts are resources that we use to help ourselves and others to be involved in spiritual warfare more effectively. Providing a detailed discussion of spiritual gifts is beyond the scope of this book. However, there is no shortage of good books that address the subject. References to several of these are in Appendix A.

The Promises we have been given in the Bible - Knowledge of promises given us in the Bible can also be a resource. Part of our knowledge of Biblical truth is learning about God's promises. We can trust God's promises and use them in spiritual warfare with confidence.[30] God is a promise-giving and a promise-keeping God. Someone has said that the entire Bible can be seen as a series of stories about how God has fulfilled the promises He has made. Many of the promises given to the Jewish nation in the Old Testament of the Bible can be accepted by Christians as also being given to them simply because the Bible says that they are the also children of Abraham by Faith.[31] The problem you can run into, however, is that many promises (especially in the Old Testament) were given to specific people for specific purposes and have specific conditions attached to them. So, we can't just find something said in the Bible that we happen to like the sound of and claim it as a promise made to us. People have done this and have come up with some pretty weird ideas about what God has "promised" them. There are many promises, however, that we can accept as intended for us as Christians even though they may have been spoken to someone else or may have conditions attached to them. We'll discuss more about this later in this chapter.

In the Hebrew language of the Old Testament, there is no special term for the concept or act of promising. Where our English translations say that someone promised something, the Hebrew simply states that someone said or spoke some word with future reference. A promise is a word that, "…goes forth into unfilled time. It reaches ahead of its speaker and its recipient, to mark an appointment between them in the future. A promise may be an assurance of continuing or future action on behalf of someone… It may be a solemn agreement of lasting, mutual (if unequal) relationship: as in the covenants. It may be the announcement of a future event…[32] In the New Testament, the word 'promise,' both as noun and verb, is used extensively. Paul found scriptural authority for his Gentile mission in God's promise to Abraham through whom all nations (i.e., Gentiles) *would be* blessed.[33] Through faith in Christ, God's promise was being fulfilled, and Gentiles were becoming Abraham's offspring[34], members of the children of promise[35] without reference to the law. The inclusion of the Gentiles, however, does not nullify God's promises to the Jews.[36] Ultimately, Jews and Gentiles will gather as one people of God.[37]

The following promises are examples of paraphrased promise statements that are especially helpful for all of us as we find ourselves involved in spiritual warfare:

- Resist the devil and he will flee from you. James 4:7

- Come near to God and He will come near to you. James 4:8

- The prayer of a righteous man is powerful and effective. James 5:16b

- Don't be afraid. I am with you. Isaiah 41:10a

- I will strengthen you and help you. I will uphold you. Isaiah 41:10b

- Our hope in God will not be disappointed. Isaiah 49:23b

- Jesus came to destroy the devil's work. 1 John 3:8b

- No weapon forged against you will prevail. Isaiah 54:17a

- We can be aware of Satan's schemes so he can't outwit us. 2 Cor. 2:11

- Our spiritual weapons have divine power. 2 Cor. 10:4

- Our power is from the Holy Spirit. Zech. 4:6b

- When two agree in prayer, it will be done. Matt. 18:19

- Ask in Jesus' name and it will be done. John 14:13-14

- There is protection and safety in Jesus' name. Prov. 18:10

- When two or more come together in Jesus' name, He is with them. Matt. 18:20

- Satan is overcome by Jesus' blood and our testimony. Rev. 12:11

- Scripture equips us for every good work. 2 Tim. 3:16-17

- Our minds are renewed as we offer ourselves to God. Rom. 12:1-2

- If you need wisdom, ask for it. James 1:5

- The Holy Spirit intercedes for us. Rom. 8:26

- Jesus is interceding for us. Rom. 8:34

- Nothing can separate us from Jesus' love. Rom. 35-39

- We are more than conquerors through Jesus. Rom. 8:37

- Victory comes through faith in Jesus. 1 John 5:4

- Jesus gives us strength to do whatever is needed. Phil. 4:13

- We are protected as we use our delegated authority. Luke 10:19

- The Lord will rescue us from evil attacks. 2 Tim. 4:18

- God will fight for and deliver us. Isaiah 49:25

- All must bow to Jesus' name. Phil. 2:9-11

- God wants bonds of wickedness loosed; heavy burdens removed; freedom for the oppressed; every yoke broken. Isaiah 58:6

- Jesus has disarmed satanic powers. Colossians 2:14-15

- God gives us the desire and power to do what pleases Him. Phil. 2:13

- Whatever you bind on earth will be bound in heaven, and whatever you loose on earth will be loosed in heaven. Matt.18:18

- You will know the truth, and the truth will set you free. John 8:32

- God's mighty power at work in us is able to do far more than we would ever dare to ask, or even dream of – infinitely beyond our highest prayers, desires, thoughts, or hopes. Ephesians 3:20

These promises are examples of God 'speaking' to us through things recorded in the Bible. God tells us that we are given these promises so that we will "purify ourselves from everything that contaminates body and spirit, perfecting holiness out of reverence for God."[38] You will remember that the word *rhema* rather than *logos* was used in Ephesians 6 to describe the Sword of the Spirit which was the Word of God. We are told that *logos* is reasoned speech and *rhema* is an utterance[39]. For example, in his announcement to the virgin Mary that she had been chosen to bring the Messiah into the world, the angel Gabriel says to her that "Nothing God says (*rhema*) is impossible." Mary says, "Let it be done to me according to your '*rhema*.'"[40] This was a disclosure from one person to another. God's promises can sometimes be '*rhema*' promises to us personally. We'll discuss that later.

Hope – The kind of 'hope' we have as Christians is not *just* a 'wish'. It is a wish, but it is so much more than just a wish. It is like the first light in the morning sky – the expectation and anticipation of a new day. This kind of hope includes a 'knowing' that the resources promised to us by God are real and active – something is about to happen! And, God will use whatever happens for our highest good.[41] In this context, hope is very closely related to faith. The difference is that hope is something that we can feel and know because God has given us the gift of faith. The Bible says, "For it is by grace [God's unmerited favor] that you have been saved, through faith – and this is not from yourselves, it is a gift of God – not by works, so that no one can boast."[42] God gives us faith so that we can experience His kind of hope. God then works through us to love and serve others. "For we are God's workmanship, created in Christ Jesus to do good works, which God prepared in advance for us to do."[43] Faith, hope, and love are a trinity of God's grace gifts to us and to others through us. They will last forever.[44]

The word *logos* is usually used to describe God's general revelation of Himself and His truth in the Scriptures – the Bible. The Bible says that, "In the past God spoke to our forefathers through the prophets at many times and in various ways[45]" – a disclosure from one person to another. So we see that the book we know as the Bible is a written record of what God spoke (revealed) to people who then recorded it. It was God's *'rhema'* revelation to the person who was to later write it down. The revelation that was written down (the Bible) is for us a *logos* revelation. In his letter to the Ephesian church, the apostle Paul wrote that he kept asking God to give them the Spirit of wisdom and revelation so that they might know God better.[46] If you have 'wisdom' based only on human knowledge without revelation, you may be open to a spirit of pride. If you have revelation without knowledge based on the truth of the scripture, you may be open to a religious spirit. If you have both knowledge and revelation you are in a much better position to also have understanding. Proverbs says we are to do everything in our power to get both wisdom and understanding[47]. If we are going to be able to effectively use the resources God has given us, we will need *both* wisdom and revelation:

> From the spirit come both wisdom and revelation. We
> need them both to walk with God, need them in generous doses
> to navigate the dangerous waters of this world. If we're the sort

of person who tends to lean toward revelation (just asking God for direct guidance), then we need to balance our approach with wisdom. If we lean toward a wisdom approach to life, we must deliberately and consciously be open to and include revelation. Ask God. And, "…if we operate for the most part, with neither, we are in real trouble… People have done a lot of really stupid things in the name of following Jesus… Don't surrender this treasure of intimacy with God just because it can get messy. Walk with God – wisdom *and* revelation – all the while seeking the holiness we know he is after."[48]

So, does God really 'speak' to people today? You bet. He really *does* speak to us today. Eldredge expresses his belief like this:

> Now, I know, I know – the prevailing belief is that God speaks to his people *only* through the Bible. And let me make this clear: he does speak to us first and foremost through the Bible. That is the basis for our relationship… any other supposed revelation from God that contradicts the Bible is not to be trusted. So I am not minimizing in any way the authority of the Scripture or the fact that God speaks to us through the Bible… However, many Christians believe that God *only* speaks to us through the Bible. The irony of that belief is that's not what the Bible says. The Bible is filled with stories of God talking to his people… Now, if God doesn't also speak to us, why would he have given us all these stories of him speaking to others? That makes no sense at all. Why would God give you a book of exceptions?[49]

Dr. Lehman also believes that God speaks to us. An indispensible part of the ministry he calls 'The Immanuel approach' involves his clients being able to 'establish real time, interactive connection in the present' with Jesus; hearing statements of truth from Jesus to deal with healing memories that contain toxic content.[50] Dr. Lehman describes this process as:

> [I am]… experiencing an *interactive* connection with the Lord when I perceive His presence in some way and it *feels* true that we are having a living, real time, mutual, contingent *interaction*… When I am experiencing an interactive connection,

it *feels* true that the Lord Jesus sees, hears, and understands the emotions and thoughts I am experiencing and communicating, and it also *feels* true that he is offering contingent responses to my emotions and thoughts…*Contingent* interaction means that our responses are directly related to (contingent upon) what the other is experiencing and communicating.[51]

I can't imagine a better description of what a *rhema* communication with the Lord would be or feel like. I personally experience this when I feel that the Lord (or the Holy Spirit) is speaking to me and guiding my thoughts; like, when some thought or idea 'jumps' out of the context of what I am reading, listening to, seeing, or just thinking about; and, sometimes, a series of thoughts or insights from two or more previously unrelated sources suddenly combine to reveal a spiritual truth or insight that is new to me. Many Christians experience this kind of 'jumping out at you' when they are reading the Scripture. For example, several years ago I was attending a church staff devotional time. We were reading from 2 Kings. In chapter 4, a man gave Elisha the prophet twenty loaves of bread. Elisha told his servant to give the loaves of bread to the people with them. The servant responded, 'How can I set this before a hundred men?" Elisha answered, "Give it to the people to eat. For this is what the Lord says: 'They will eat and have some left over.'" (Verses 42-44). As I was reading this, I was also struggling with concerns about how my wife and I could possibly survive financially with only our Social Security income after my planned retirement. At that moment, I 'heard' an inaudible voice in my spirit telling me that 'we were not to worry about our finances – that there would always be enough and some left over'. This was, to use Dr. Lehman's words, a 'contingent interaction' from the Lord responding precisely to my concerns at that moment. It was not a license to be foolish with our finances. But, when our faith weakens and concerns surface, we always come back to that special promise to us. It was a *rhema* promise for my wife and me - one that has proven to be absolutely true. Remember, always check any *rhema* revelation against scriptural truth. The Bible says basically the same thing[52] so it clearly fits with Biblical truth but, somehow, it felt so much more real to me to 'hear' it in that way. By the way, don't ask for or expect a *rhema* communication from God for things or truths that are already addressed clearly in the Bible. I believe that this kind of hearing from God (*rhema*) is what is behind several of the spiritual gifts (word of knowledge, word of wisdom, discerning of spirits, interpretation of tongues, special faith, etc.).

You may be wondering in what ways God might 'speak' to you. There are many, many ways: reading and studying the Bible, reading books, through teachings, through counselors and mentors, through movies, through epic stories like Tolkien's *The Lord of The Rings*, or C. S. Lewis' *The Chronicles of Narnia*, through songs, through the things family and friends (and even strangers) say, through the way our pets relate to us, through the example of others (sometimes good and sometimes bad), even through cartoons in the paper. The list is endless. Of course, the primary source of receiving revelation from God is through the Bible. When I 'hear' a message that I feel might be a *rhema* message from God, I write it down as soon as I can along with any questions I might have about it. Sometimes I get just a few words at a time, and then hear more at a later time (hours, days, or weeks). The important part is to write down what you feel you have heard. The things God says to you are far too important to trust to memory alone – even if you don't understand what it means to start with. John Eldredge gives two additional and important words of caution: First, when you get a partial (*rhema*) word from God, don't just charge ahead and start filling in the blanks with your own imagination or reasoning (as most of us tend to do). Ask God for more detail – what, how, when kinds of questions. Then wait for the answers. Second, as you are waiting for answers to the additional questions, pay attention to your own mental posture. What are your feelings? What are your desires? We have to be willing to hear what God has to say, respond to it, and not let what *we* want to hear bias what we do hear.[53] A basic knowledge of Biblical truth and principles is the absolutely fundamental prerequisite for deciding whether or not to accept a (*rhema*) word from God regardless of the source. It is always wise and helpful to bounce any 'special word' or 'insight' from the Lord that you feel you have heard off a friend whom you know to be a mature Christian and well versed in the Biblical truth – especially if you are new to this kind of communication with God.

Getting *rhema* words (revelations) from God is like finding large gold nuggets in a grassy field. You don't have to dig for them but you do have to pick them up (receive them). Also, be careful not to step in the 'spiritual' cow pies in that same grassy field. Choose the good and the true – avoid the bad and the false.

If you are a Christian who is not currently experiencing communication with God in this intimate, personal way and you would like to, you might start by getting John Eldredge's book *"Walking with God"* and read it carefully and prayerfully. Then, also, do as I did and get the companion *"Walking with God Workbook"* and go through it. I can almost guarantee that it will be a life-changing experience for you. It was for me.

Fruit of the Spirit – The fruit of the Spirit includes: love, joy, peace, patience, kindness, goodness, gentleness, and self-control.[54] Although not strictly resources for spiritual warfare, these are characteristics of a Christian who is living his or her life in the power of and under the direction of the Holy Spirit. Any person displaying these characteristics will certainly be more effective and successful as he or she wages spiritual warfare than one who doesn't. These are characteristics that will become progressively more obvious in our lives as we become more and more like Jesus. Romans 8:29 says that this is our ultimate destiny as Christians.

The first fruit of the Holy Spirit is love. This is a special kind of love. The Greek word used for this kind of love is *agape*. It is the kind of love that God has for each of us and that we will personally display as we become more and more like Him. The Bible tells us what this kind of love looks like: "Love is patient, love is kind. It does not envy, it does not boast. It is not rude, it is not self-seeking. It is not easily angered, it keeps no record of wrongs. Love does not delight in evil but rejoices with the truth. It always protects, always hopes, always perseveres. Love never fails."[55] All of our resources need to be used in the context of God's *agape* love; both toward ourselves and others. The Bible says that the only thing that counts is faith expressing itself through love.[56]

The Holy Spirit – The Holy Spirit is God living in us. He is not just a resource – He is the source of all our resources. Someone has said that we become like a Swiss army knife in the hands of the Holy Spirit. Most Christians have no idea what incredibly great power they are capable of wielding when they battle Satan in Jesus' name. I'm reminded of a drawing I've seen of a kitten looking into a mirror. The refection the kitten sees in the mirror is a huge lion looking back at him. That reflection reminds me of my mental image of Aslan (the lion representation of Jesus) in C. S. Lewis' *The Lion the Witch and the Wardrobe*. We are the kitten. Who we are in Jesus is the lion! I hope you are now starting to get a better grasp of this truth. As Christians, we are superbly equipped to both live the Christian life and to do battle with evil in Jesus' name. We now know what many of our resources are. In the next three chapters, we will learn more about how to use these weapons against the evil forces of darkness trying to influence our lives.

There is so much more to be said about the Holy Spirit. He could be the subject of this whole book and has been the primary subject of many books. If you would like to learn more about the Holy Spirit – Who He is and how He works in our lives, I recommend Jerry Cook's little book, *The Holy Spirit, So…What's The Big Deal?*[57]

Limitations - We want to be as effective as possible when we are opposing the enemy in our own lives or those of others. Is there anything that can limit or block our ability to effectively use our delegated authority, power, position, and our other resources? Unfortunately, Yes! The whole focus of demonic efforts is to damage our fellowship with God and, by doing so, block the effectiveness of our use of the resources God has given us to help ourselves and others. God will not overrule our free-will choices. We can choose to live in a way that will limit or completely neutralize our ability to use our spiritual resources.

Things that can limit our effectiveness in walking the Christian life and in waging spiritual warfare include:

- Footholds and strongholds (which we will cover in later chapters)

- Memories that need to be healed (which we will cover in a later chapter)

- Unconfessed sin in our lives (including sins of omission) - things like unforgiveness of others or ourselves, bitterness, laziness, complacency, pornography, addictions, etc. The list could go on forever. I will treat 'unforgiveness' as a special category of sin because Jesus made a special point of saying that, if we don't forgive others, we won't be forgiven.[58] However, when we look at everything that the scripture has to say about sin, we will realize that this is true of any known sin in our lives. We are to deal with sin we become aware of (regardless of the source or what sin it is) in one primary way: repentance and confession; and, then, to use our other spiritual resources as needed. The Bible says that, if we'll confess the sin we know about, God will take care of (forgive) all the sin we don't know about.[59] Let me express this in another way. If our heart attitude and commitment is to confess sin when we become aware of it, then the sin we are unaware of is already forgiven!

Many have asked why should we be required to confess our sin if Jesus already paid for all sin – actually, the sin of the whole world?[60] There is a two-part answer to this important question. First, our sin causes us to lose our *fellowship* with God. Our *relationship* with God is secure but, when we allow sin to continue in our lives, we lose our fellowship with God – that recognition of His presence with us and feeling of His closeness to us. The second part of the answer deals with the other consequences of known sin in our lives (which are really just associated with losing our fellowship with God). These   from us[62], keeping God from hearing our prayers[63], not measuring up to God's standard of perfect righteousness[64], keeping us from pleasing God[65] and, ending up in slavery to sin by establishing footholds (areas of demonic influence in our lives).[66] Joshua 7:13 says that we can't stand before our enemies until we remove sin. This statement was applied to actual warfare but it also applies to spiritual warfare.

- Unforgiveness.

Forgiveness must be a central reality of all relationships. "We live outside the garden (of Eden) and, all around us, a war of enormous proportion is being waged against our souls – a war of abuse that pits us against the lion who seeks to damage and devour our lives." Dan Allender goes on to write:

… We will see the importance of forgiveness as a central category in relating to others to the extent that we see every relationship enmeshed in a war that leads to a taste of heaven or hell. If we understand the battle we are engaged in and the nature of the wounds we experience, forgiveness is seen as the foundation for comprehending the goodness of God and the only hope for restored relationships with others. ...forgiveness becomes more necessary to the degree the damage of living in a fallen world is faced. ...The terrain of the eternal war is the battleground of relationships. ...The war against us is disguised behind the humdrum monotony and imperceptible abuses of daily living ...[67]

The wounds we receive from others may seem inconsequential or they may seem devastating - either way, they accumulate. Refusing to forgive is like being sentenced to 'death by a thousand cuts'. Unforgiveness eats away at us from within. Someone has said that refusing to forgive is like us taking poison and expecting the other person to get sick. Someone else has said that forgiveness is like setting a prisoner free and then discovering that the prisoner was us.

We also need to be aware that the old saying 'Forgive and Forget' is an attempt by Satan to create a false illusion that, once forgiveness is offered, everything is then okay and the relationship should immediately go back to the way it was before the offense. This fosters the potential for continued destructive behavior patterns on the part of both the wrongdoer and the one wronged. The Bible tells us that David avoided future abuse, including the threat of death, from King Saul by leaving Jerusalem and hiding in the wilderness. David's act of self-preservation by fleeing in the face of real danger, while at the same time, refusing to yield to the urge to retaliate, is a model for dealing with abusive people in our own lives.[68]

Unforgiveness is sin and we need to recognize it for what it is and deal with it like any other sin – confession and repentance. Sometimes, forgiving seems easy. Sometimes, it seems almost impossible. Many fine books have been written about forgiveness. One of the best is the book *Bold Love*.[69] If you are having difficulty dealing with unforgiveness, I encourage you to get *Bold Love* and thoughtfully read it.

- Lack of knowledge of truth – including ignorance of Satan's strategies.

    The old saying that what you don't know can't hurt you is a saying that is just plain wrong! One of the reasons for writing this book is so people can understand more of what is happening to them so they won't be blindsided by "what they don't know" and taken out by the enemy of our souls. Spiritual darkness can exist only in the absence of spiritual truth. I want to encourage you to learn all you can about the truth God has revealed in the Bible. There are many really good books that will help you learn Biblical truth. I've included a list of several of them in Appendix A.

- Generational influences in our lives

    In the context of stating the Ten Commandments, the Bible says that God is a jealous God and will, "…visit the iniquity of the fathers on the children for the sin of the fathers to the third and fourth generation of those who hate me, but showing love to thousands who love me and keep my commandments."[70] How can a God of justice punish a person for someone else's sin? Is it really fair to punish children for the sins of their fathers? The Bible says that, God holds each one of us accountable for our own sin: "The soul who sins shall die. The son shall not suffer for the iniquity of the father nor the father suffer for the iniquity of the son."[71] God never condemns the innocent - only the guilty. Are these verses in conflict? No. It is important to notice something in the second commandment that is often overlooked, namely, how the threat ends. God says that he will punish three or four generations '… of those who hate me.' It is not just the fathers who hate God, but also their children. People who struggle with the fairness of this commandment usually assume that although the father is guilty, his children are innocent. But, the children will be punished only if they hate God as the father did, which, given the way they were raised, would not be surprising. Therefore, it would be fair and just for God to punish the children for their own sin. God also promises to show mercy to those who love him and keep his commandments. This promise is more powerful than the warning because it's a blessing that lasts not just for three or four generations, but for a thousand; in other words, it will last forever.

There is, however, a way in which generational sins can affect us because our parent's and ancestor's sins do have consequences that can last for generations. Specific sin patterns do tend to run in families because children tend to imitate their parents and believe those things (including the lies) that their parents believed. One generation sets the spiritual tone for the next. So, perhaps the second commandment warning is based on universal truths about family relationships.[72] For example, adult children of alcoholics suffer the consequences of being raised in that environment. Also, they may inherit a genetic predisposition toward alcoholism. For this reason, we do need to acknowledge and break the influence that generational sins have had in our lives. Also, we need to forgive our parents and our ancestors for the sinful influences and tendencies that have been passed on to us.

One more thought: though we have no guilt for the sins of our parents, we do have a responsibility to do what we can to correct the negative consequences of their sins in our own lives or the lives of others. For example, allowing slavery in America was both an individual and national sin. No one living in America today is responsible for that sin. But, we do need to do what we reasonably can to deal with its consequences.

- Not being under authority

We have already seen that allowing known sin in our lives can separate us from our fellowship with God. The Bible also tells us that we are to be in submission to both civil and spiritual authority that God has established.[73] When we don't do this, we sin and incur the consequences. The only exception to this principal is when that authority requires us to do something that directly conflicts with what the Bible clearly requires.

- Speaking 'curses' on ourselves or others.

Proverbs 18:21 says that the tongue has the power of life and death. Jesus said that whatever we bind on earth will be bound in heaven and whatever we loose on earth will be loosed in heaven.[74] This verse is really valuable when we need to 'bind' the works of evil as part of spiritual warfare. But, in a way, it is a double edged sword. We can speak curses on ourselves or others and give our enemy the right to attack us or them by what we say or agree with. A curse is saying something 'evil' against ourselves or others. For example, "You are (or I am) so stupid" or "You (or I) will never measure up or amount to anything." Most of us have spoken or heard statements like these said. When we agree with statements like these, we establish strongholds in our lives that make us more vulnerable to temptation and sin in our lives. When we sin, we give Satan a place of influence in our lives[75] and establish footholds (see Chapter five). You can choose to simply reject curses spoken to or about you. Agree with curses or reject them - It is up to you. Choose to be a person who speaks blessings to others and yourself – not curses! By the way, some people take this truth way too far and become fearful to speak anything that might sound 'negative' even if it is the truth and intended to be helpful. Be careful not to get caught in that trap.

- Overuse or misuse of our strengths

We each have abilities in our lives that we recognize as strengths as well as some things we recognize as weaknesses. When we make 'idols' of our strengths or over-use or miss-use our strengths, they will often then be seen by others as weaknesses and may be hurtful or offensive to others. This can damage our relationships and limit our ability to be used by God to be a blessing to them. For example, if you have the strength of being persuasive, and you over-use or miss-use it, you might be seen by others as being manipulative. Or, if you are too analytical, you might be seen as being critical or judgmental. When we use our strengths in a way that hurts ourselves or others, we need to recognize that we are sinning. This kind of sin has the same dangerous consequences as any other kind of sin. We may be tempted to think we have a particular area of knowledge or skill 'down pat'. This can cause us to rush into a situation in our *own* strength (using our own natural abilities or resources) without appropriate caution or preparation. When we do this, we are in danger of making serious mistakes or doing real damage. This is especially true when we are engaging in spiritual warfare.

The Bible tells us to, "…throw off everything that hinders and the sin that so easily entangles, and let us run with perseverance the race marked out for us."[76] When we recognize any of these limitations in our lives, we need to deal with them immediately. The last thing we want is to not have access to our spiritual resources and find ourselves vulnerable to spiritual attack. Others can, and often will, see things that we can't (especially our spouses). If we will listen to them, they can help us focus on things we need to deal with. When we actually start to use our resources in spiritual warfare, we might be tempted to be a 'lone wolf'. Don't fight alone! Get help. Find others who understand the kind of spiritual warfare this book talks about and ask them to join you in the battle. All of us need a "band of warriors" to fight and work together with us. Jesus said that, where two or more agree about anything we ask for (according to His will), it will be done for us by our Father in heaven.[77]

Allowing known sin to continue in our lives always leads to bondage to satanic influence. We will learn more about this bondage and how to get free from it in the next chapter.

FOOTHOLDS

"I tell you the truth, everyone who sins is a slave to sin.[1]" Jesus

Most of us first begin to recognize that things are not going the way they 'should' in our lives because we keep thinking or doing things that, at some level of our awareness, we know are wrong. We often resolve to do 'better' in the future but rarely do for any length of time. Usually, we notice that these things we think or do have a 'compulsive' nature about them. "I just can't help being angry." "I can't stop being fearful, or bitter, or …" "Why is my life strewn with so many broken relationships?" We may wonder why even as we continue to do them. These 'problems' in our lives may start out as minor annoyances, but over time, they can become major problems – if not for us, then, for those who have to live with us. A little temper problem, for example, can slowly change into a reason for divorce or, perhaps, verbal, physical, or emotional abuse. What's going on?

We were introduced to footholds in chapter two. We learned that allowing sin in our lives has horrific consequences. When we sin, we give the devil a "foothold" (a place of influence in our life related to that particular sin). The longer we continue to sin in a particular way, the greater that demonic influence becomes. Once we have begun to sin repeatedly in a particular area, It becomes like a habit, a compulsion, or an addiction. We all end up with satanic footholds (areas of bondage) in our lives. Demonic spirits will use these limited areas of control in our lives to keep us sinning if we allow them to. These evil spirits want us to experience the terrible consequences of sin and, especially, the loss of our *fellowship* with God. When that happens, we become 'easy pickings' for them. To use an old saying, we 'go from the frying pan into the fire'. The good news is that, if we are truly Christians, no evil spirit can sever our *relationship* with God. Only we can do that. But, sin does disrupt our *fellowship* with God. All this should sound familiar and make sense to you. If not, go back and review chapter two and the last part of chapter three. You might also ask a mature Christian friend who understands these truths to help you understand more clearly.

As Christians, we usually know that we need to confess our sin to re-establish our fellowship with God. However, relatively few Christians today are taught that sin opens us up to bondage to a demonic spirit. So, we repent and confess our sin with every intention of not sinning in that way again. Then, we find ourselves doing just that. We confess again and again and the cycle of sin and confession continues even as we become more and more discouraged and depressed. Eventually, we often just quit trying. The problem is that we are dealing with specific occurrences of sin by our confession but we are not dealing with the bondage (foothold) we have given to a powerful spiritual enemy. Once we have gotten rid of the foothold, the compulsive, driven, power that sin has over us is removed and it is much easier to keep from repeating it. If we do repeat it, we give back the foothold. But, hopefully, we will recognize immediately what we have done. Then, we can confess that sin again and then get rid of the bondage we have re-established.

We have said that strongholds are what set us up to be drawn into bondage. Just how does that happen? Sometimes we simply choose to sin - knowing that we are doing it. And, of course, this establishes bondage in the area in which we choose to sin. But, just as often, we get carried away with the emotions we have as a result of past hurtful experiences. We need to be very clear that our emotions are wonderful gifts from God. But, just like God's other good gifts of grace in our lives, if we overuse or misuse them, they can be used in sinful ways.

Hurtful things happen to us all. When they do, we feel the emotions associated with what happened to us: anger, disappointment, fear, panic depression... Strong emotions like these can even come from normal, everyday experiences. If a hurtful experience has been fully processed and something happens that reminds us of that experience, we will remember and accept the emotions we felt at that time and use them to motivate us to take appropriate actions. If we have not completely processed a hurtful experience, we tend to accept and believe the false conclusions our minds came up with to explain the experience along with the related emotions or feelings about what happened. Then, we file it all away in our 'implicit' (unconscious) memory. When we are triggered (i.e., when we experience something that awakens those memories and feelings), we will react to these buried emotions from the past inappropriately - as though they were caused by whatever triggered them in the present. When for any reason (fear of authority figures, other beliefs, etc.), we don't feel free to express the primary emotions we first felt, we may then feel secondary emotions that seem less threatening. For example, if our primary emotion was fear, or panic, or anger at injustice, we might choose to feel sadness, or depression, or, perhaps, a desire to escape. We might lash out with a degree of intensity that is completely inappropriate for whatever it was that triggered our response. We might or might not express any emotion openly depending on the situation. Any response that is not based on "truth in love" is sin and will establish a new foothold or strengthen an existing one.

In addition to experiencing emotions based on a lie, there is another way we can get in trouble from believing a stronghold. When we have established a stronghold, we also establish a set of expectations based on the lie we believed. We all tend to see and experience what we expect to see and experience. Usually these expectations are based on our past experiences, so they are not entirely unreasonable. The problem is that not every person or every situation will actually be like what we experienced in the past – but we tend to act as though it is. We assume that the expectation our mind created to explain past toxic experiences will be true in the present situation. We then tend to behave as though what we expected to see or experience has actually been experienced even though it has not. For example, if we expect that others will not really be there for us, or will reject us, or are not able or willing to meet our needs, then we will almost always treat them as though this was actually happening whether it has or not. When we treat others like that, it is no wonder that they respond to us in the way we expected. Our expectation has become a self-fulfilling prophesy. Other's responses to us confirm our expectations, we continue to react, and the downward spiral of damaged relationships accelerates.

Strongholds and the related emotions or expectations interact with and reinforce each other. When we allow our emotions and our expectations to control our behavior, we will almost certainly hurt and alienate others. When we do this, we have sinned again and established a new foothold or strengthened an existing one.

How can we avoid this? Sometimes we simply can't because the stronghold, emotions, or expectations are buried in our subconscious mind. There is little we can do except to experience the negative consequences and wonder why things happen the way they did. If we are in touch with our strongholds (aware of our emotions, and expectations - which we rarely are), we can ask God to help us deal with them. If we will listen, the Holy Spirit can remind us that we must not react to a hurtful memory from the past; that every person and every situation is different. He can help us realize that we have been triggered by something in the present and that we are being tempted to react to something that actually happened to us in the past. God can (and will, if we let him) remind us to set our personal emotions and expectations aside and listen to the other person. We need to try to understand what is actually happening in the present and not be lured into sinful behaviors. As we do that, the chances of our being able to respond in a loving, respectful way, are greatly improved. The situation may or may not be resolved. But, at least, we won't be responsible for pouring more fuel on the fire of conflict and misunderstanding. At least we will have tried, as much as it is up to us, to create a more loving, trusting and caring atmosphere. That is the best any of us can do.

Once we do realize that we have opened the door to demonic influence in our lives by giving footholds to evil spirits, most of us are more than ready to do whatever is needed to get rid of them. Here is some more good news: God has given us the spiritual resources we need to get rid of footholds in our lives. I was first exposed to a simple tool to use as a guide in the process of getting rid of footholds through Cleansing Stream Ministries.2 This tool involves four words that start with the letter 'R': revelation, repentance, renouncing, and restoration. Each word represents a step in the process.

The 'revelation' step involves recognizing that we have a specific area in our life that is getting or has gotten out of control – we have been sinning in a specific way. We recognize that we have given place to anger, or unforgiveness, or bitterness, or fear, or some kind of abuse of ourselves or others, or addiction, or…. This first step in the process also includes realizing that what we are doing is wrong and needs to be removed from our lives. If we allow it to continue, there will be serious consequences that we want to avoid. We may also become aware of the compulsive nature of what we are doing. At some level of our awareness, we might want to continue what we are doing because it is pleasurable, but, at the same time, we know it has to stop. It sounds like we are talking about an addiction – and, in a way, we are. Addictions include some 'pay-off' (some 'reward') that keeps us doing it. In the case of sin, the same is true. Also, just like an addiction, sin never satisfies for long and it takes more and more to get the same affect. The Bible acknowledges that "sin *is* pleasurable for a short time"3 but it is just a substitute for what will really satisfy us. We'll talk more about that later. The problem is the price we have to pay to continue it.

As we approach getting rid of footholds we are usually aware of several areas of bondage that we know we should deal with. The first thing we need to do is ask God which He wants us to deal with first. Some footholds can be dealt with more easily than others. Some areas of bondage need to be removed before others will yield to being removed. God knows the order in which each needs to be removed. So, ask Him. You will soon have a sense which to start with. He might even say, "Start where ever you want." Once you decide where to start, get rid of each in turn. Go through all four steps of the process for each area of sin (each foothold) one at a time.

The 'repentance' step in the process involves turning away from the sin we have recognized. Repentance means turning around and going the other way with the sincere intent not to repeat the same sinful behavior. We've been moving away from God so, right where we are; we turn and start moving back toward Him. We do this by agreeing with our conscience and with the conviction prompted within us by the Holy Spirit that what we have been doing is sin. We discussed receiving forgiveness from God, and giving forgiveness to others and to ourselves in chapter three. As an aside, the 'conviction' we feel from the Holy Spirit is not 'condemnation'. Condemnation comes from the devil and is intended to discourage us and turn us away from God. Conviction comes from God and is intended to draw us back into fellowship with Him through confession. Again, if these concepts are not clear, go back and review the earlier chapters where these things are discussed. We'll cover the kinds of words you might want to use to do this later in this chapter.

The 'renouncing' step involves using the resources God has given us to break the demonic bondage that has been established by our sin. After we have confessed our sin, our fellowship with God is re-established but the demonic influence still needs to be dealt with. Renouncing means to tell the demonic entity that, in Jesus' name and in His authority, we take back our freedom and the control we gave away in this area of our life; that the demonic influence no longer has any right to try to control or influence us in this area; that we break his influence over us. Just as a reminder, we speak out loud as we do this. Satan and his helpers don't know for sure what we are thinking until we speak it verbally because they can't read our mind. The ability to know what Christians are thinking is reserved only for our own minds and the Holy Spirit who lives in us. Speaking out loud is the only way to be sure they hear what we are declaring and commanding. We are not asking God to do this. God has given us the authority, the power, and the responsibility to do this. We don't need to do this in a fearful or submissive way either. We are regents, ambassadors, and priests of almighty God. We don't *ask* demonic spirits to do anything – we *command* them in Jesus name – not flippantly, or haughtily, or arrogantly but simply because of who we are in Jesus.

If you have someone with you as you go through this process, ask them to agree with what you have just done and anoint you with oil after you have finished renouncing the demonic influence and taken back the ground you gave the enemy. The oil is simply a symbol of the Holy Spirit's power and involvement. It is a statement that you know whose power has accomplished what has just been done.

The 'restoration' step simply involves affirming that, by God's grace and power, we choose to be and act the opposite of the way we were being and acting under the influence of our sin nature and the demonic influence. It also involves asking God to heal any brokenness in our lives because of the foothold we have just broken.

This process might sound complicated but it really is not. I've included an outline of the things you might want to say as you go through the process. These suggested prayers are intended to give you an idea of the kinds of things you might want to say. These prayers are not intended to be formulas or used in any 'ritual' way.

Revelation (from God)

Lord, please show me clearly the area of sin I have committed that You want to deal with next. . Please give me the ability to wait patiently until I receive of Your guidance. Please give me the courage and wisdom to proceed through this process step by step with your guidance. Lord, if You are not part of this process, I don't want any part of it either.

Repent (to God):

Father, I come before You acknowledging the sin of ….. (unforgiveness, sexual sin, shame, anger, fear of failure, fear of life (undirected fear), bitterness, selfishness, rebellion, addiction, control, pride, self hatred, …) in my life. I repent for giving in to (name the sin) and allowing the enemy access to my life. I turn away from it now. By Your grace, I choose not to continue repeating this sin. I repent for how I have treated others because of (name the sin). I forgive anyone whom I have blamed for 'causing' me to sin in this way – including those in my former generations. Where my generations before me have partnered with (name the sin), I confess this generational sin and ask for Your grace to flow to me and my family. Thank you for forgiving and cleansing me. I don't want anything to come between us. I ask this in Jesus Name.

Renounce (taking back the place we have given to the enemy – out loud with our eyes open):

I renounce (name the sin). I renounce all spirits behind it and bind them in Jesus' name from supporting each other in any way. I hate what you have done in my life to rob, kill, and destroy my fellowship with my Lord. I declare that I am free from your power. Everything I have said or done that has given you any place in my life, I renounce and cancel. I refuse to accept your influence, intimidation, or manipulation in my life any longer. In the name of Jesus, I close all doors I have opened to (name the sin) and I seal those doors shut with the blood of Jesus. I refuse to believe your lies and I stand by faith upon God's word. The Lord is my strength and my hope. I break all word curses, vows, covenants, and agreements, known or unknown, that either I or my past generations have made that have given you any access, power, or influence in my life. I take back every place I have given you in my life. I command you to get out of my life – leave me now! I choose to give God this place of rulership in my life. I do this in the mighty name of Jesus!

Restoration (healing from God)

Lord, I ask you to restore my life and my heart from any and all damage because of my involvement with (name the sin). I ask you Holy Spirit to enter and fill this place in me. I invite you to rule and reign in my life. Lord, I ask you to bless me with boldness and confidence to trust you. Father God, I open my heart to receive Your unconditional love, grace, forgiveness, and the full release from (name the sin) in my life. And, by Your grace and power, I choose to be a person who is (whatever is opposite of the sin being dealt with).

There is another type of bondage that most of us will also need to deal with. The church's term for this kind of bondage is "soul tie". The term soul tie is used to summarize several terms used in the Bible like 'knit', 'cleave', and 'joined' - in other words, strong connections. A soul tie is a place of control or influence in our soul. By our 'soul', we mean our mind, emotions, and will. A soul tie is really a special kind of a foothold; but one that is based on connections we establish with a person or object. There are good soul ties and bad soul ties. Good soul ties include connections that are based on wholesome relationships – like those that can exist between God and us, a husband and a wife, parents and children, friend to friend, a leader and those who follow, a counselor and counselee, readers and an author, us and our favorite book or Bible, fond memories of a place,… Bad soul ties include connections that are based on unwholesome or sinful relationships – like those associated with various forms of abuse (verbal, emotional, physical, sexual,…), manipulation, coercion, dishonesty, various forms of voyeurism (like pornography, sexting, 'romance' novels, internet or phone sex, characters or situations in movies or on TV, a flirtatious, emotional 'affair' at the office or elsewhere,…), leaders of cults or the cults themselves - any connection or relationship that establishes dependencies on or connections with anything other than, or in the place of, God in our souls. These connections become "imprinted" on us with good or bad consequences because we tend to 'take on' the characteristics of those people and things that we have strong physical or emotional connections with. For example, Christians become (or should become) more like Jesus3; Husbands and wives often take on each other's mannerisms, way of speaking, likes and dislikes. These connections can take place at a spiritual level too. The Bible tells us that a husband and wife, for example, "become one flesh" from God's perspective.5 That is why sexually oriented sin can create such serious problems in the lives of those involved. Bad soul ties (sinful connections) allow demonic spirits to influence our behavior and spiritual walk – to try to get us to accept the same spiritual hang-ups, perversions, and footholds of those we are or have been connected with. It is not unusual for us to find ourselves compulsively thinking about, fanaticizing about, or replaying the thoughts or actions in our mind that led to the establishment of the bad soul tie. When we find ourselves doing this, it is a clear indication that we have established a bad soul tie that needs to be broken. So, what can we do about these bondages? We can do the same thing we do with other footholds – get rid of them!

Ask Jesus to help you remember any unwholesome relationship that established a bad soul tie. As the memories of these relationships or connections occur to you, write them down on a list. If you don't remember specific names or details, just write down a word or two to remind you of the situation ("the date rape in high school", "the girl at the bar", "the guy at the office",…). This is the 'revelation' step in getting rid of these connections. Then, proceed as you would with any other foothold – entry by entry, confess your sin related to each thing on your list; renounce and break all spiritual connections associated with each person or thing on the list; and, finally, ask God to heal and restore your soul from all the damage done by these connections. When you're all done, tear up the list into little pieces and throw it away. If you remember anything else later that you think needs to be dealt with, just follow the same process. The important thing is that you seek forgiveness, freedom, and restoration for what you do remember – not that you drive yourself crazy trying to remember every possible bad soul tie. I believe that the same principal applies to dealing with bad soul ties as to any other sin in our lives – God cares about our heart attitude. Confess the stuff we know about and God will forgive and deal with all the rest.5

Recognize that, even though the foothold is gone, the habit of the sinful behavior related to it will usually still be there. The difference now is that behaving in a Godly way will be much easier because you won't have the demonically driven compulsion related to the foothold. The Bible says that we are to "resist the devil and he will flee from us"7. We also need to consistently resist the habitual tendency too. Over time, the habit will be broken too and, most of the time, even the temptation to sin in that same way will no longer be a problem. We'll discuss dealing with our sinful habits in chapter ___, Staying Free.

One of the best ways to get help in breaking the bondage of footholds is to find a church in your area that sponsors the Cleansing Stream Seminars. You will receive several weeks of video teachings covering the things you need to know as you break footholds and strongholds in small group settings. Then, you will attend a one-day retreat that will show you exactly how to do this for yourself and give you actual experience doing it. Just go to their website (www.cleansingstream.org). Contact Cleansing Stream Ministries to get a list of the churches that are sponsoring seminars in your area and for the retreat schedule. Then call the local church to find out when the Cleansing Stream seminar sessions are scheduled - usually, over a period of several weeks, twice a year.

Once you've gotten rid of the known areas of sin and bondage in your life, the next step is to discover and deal with the lies you believed that set you up to fall prey to that sin and bondage in the first place. When we focus on footholds without dealing with the strongholds behind them we are focusing on symptoms and not fixing the causes. It is like taking medication to relieve a chronic headache and not dealing with the tumor in our brain. The 'fix' is only temporary. If we don't fix the cause (a stronghold), sooner or later we'll just re-establish the related foothold again. We are rarely aware of the strongholds or memories behind our pain and bondage. We just know we want to get rid of our pain. Discovering and dealing with strongholds is the subject of the next ___chapters.

Strongholds

(This is a very long chapter that should probably be broken up into several shorter chapters.)

Strongholds – part 1 - WHAT WE'VE LEARNED SO FAR (possible chapter title?)

If we will be effective in spiritual warfare, the first field of conflict where we must learn warfare is in the battleground of the mind.... For the territory of the uncrucified thought-life is the beachhead of satanic assault in our lives. To defeat the devil, we must be renewed in the spirit of our minds!1

To renew your mind is to involve yourself in the process of allowing God to bring to the surface lies that you have mistakenly accepted and replace them with truth.[2]

Wherever a stronghold exists, it is a demonically induced pattern of thinking. Specifically, it is a "house made of thoughts" which has become a dwelling place for satanic activity.[3]

In chapter two, we learned that strongholds are deceptions, lies, and half-truths that are lying just below our consciousness – just waiting like landmines to be triggered. In December of 2012, my gall bladder ruptured. It was silently producing gall stones for who knows how long and finally became infected - like a time-bomb that could explode at any time and finally did. It almost killed me! Lies from the enemy can be like that because we are usually not consciously aware of them till they do damage in our lives.

The Bible says that there are three primary sources of temptation: the world, the flesh, and the devil. Our own sin nature is what the Bible calls our "flesh". The "world" includes several other sources of temptation. First, there are other people's sin-natures and their beliefs that can draw us away from what we know is right and into what we may or may not recognize is wrong. These temptations can be very subtle or very obvious. Others can also be used either consciously or unconsciously by Satan to create, or make use of, strongholds we have already developed. The "world" also includes the full array of cultural influences that can lead us to believe things that are not true that can result in our intentionally or unintentionally doing things that are wrong. Psalm 51:6 says God desires truth in our innermost parts. Satan tries to get us to focus on anything but the truth and tries to get us to believe his lies whenever possible. Jesus said that Satan "…was a murder from the beginning, not holding to the truth, for there is no truth in him. When he lies, he speaks his native language, for he is a liar and the father of lies."[4] Dr. Paul Joseph Goebbels, who was Adolf Hitler's Propaganda Minister, is usually given credit for saying, "A lie told often enough will eventually be believed". You can be sure that Satan is taking every opportunity to lie to us as often and in as many ways as he can. Remember also that Satan is called "the god of this world". He is temporarily in control of the world's political and cultural systems. He and his demonic helpers are doing everything they can to indoctrinate us into seeing things from their perspective and, either knowingly or unknowingly, joining them in their rebellion against God. Strongholds can simply be ideas, half-truths, or information presented as 'truth' that is not. When we make an agreement with a lie, we are establishing a stronghold regardless of where it came from. Strongholds make us more vulnerable to temptation, which leads us into sin, which establishes a foothold, which results in bondage to that particular sin in that area of our lives. What is even worse, the strongholds we believe almost always, in one way or another, get applied to God and limit our ability to really trust Him, to live life consistently in His presence, and to feel His love and approval.

The most insidious thing about strongholds is that they usually operate without our realizing that we are being affected by them. In other words, they are in a "blind-spot" of our awareness and set us up to be "blind-sided" by the world, the flesh, or the Devil! It's pretty easy to maintain a blind spot that we don't know we have and maybe even don't want to know we have. It's amazing how easy it is to be fooled when were fooling ourselves and we want to be fooled. Strongholds inhibit effective brain functioning, evaluation of thoughts, and decision making about appropriate behaviors, opening us up to sinning in ways that we might not even recognize that we are sinning.

Both our biological brain and our soul (spiritual mind, will, and emotions) can harbor lies and partial-truths. For this reason, the spiritual mind (our soul) can have only limited control over the appetites, desires, and urgings of the biological brain and body because it too is infected by strongholds and footholds. But, once we become Christians, our spirit comes back to life (we are 'born again' and our soul (spiritual mind, emotions, and will) can be in control if we are willing to allow God's Spirit through our spirit to progressively make us more like Jesus.

Strongholds are usually like bird's nests - made from sticks, string, feathers and whatever else is available. In the same way, strongholds are woven together from whatever we have chosen to believe from many different sources. When we allow God to direct us in the process of dealing with a few of the key inter-related lies, the whole nest of lies can sometimes come tumbling down. If we (in our own wisdom and strength) pull out a random stick or string here or there from our 'nest', we may or may not be able to significantly damage the nest and it will remain hidden in our mind waiting to get us in further trouble. All of us have more than one nest of lies that needs to be dealt with.

Strongholds – part 2 -HOW WE ESTABLISH STRONGHOLDS
(Possible chapter title?)

A lot of our beliefs about ourselves and the world come from the things we were led to believe as children. Children accept words spoken to them much more eagerly than adults. These early seeds can form vast root systems of beliefs that either help us or hurt us as we grow up[5]. The things we are told can help us recognize lies and avoid establishing strongholds (as I hope this book is doing), or, they can set us up to believe lies and establish strongholds. John Eldredge has written,

"I've made agreements without ever knowing it. By "agreements" I mean those subtle convictions we come to, ascent to, give way to, or are raised to assume are true. It happens down deep in our souls, where our real beliefs about life are formed. Something or someone whispers it to us, *life is never going to turn out the way you'd hoped, or nobody's going to come through, or God has forsaken you.* And, something in us responds, *that's true.* We make an agreement with it, and a conviction is formed. It seems so reasonable. I think we come to more of our beliefs in this way than maybe any other. Subtle agreements."[6]

We also need to be careful about how we deal with suffering and other painful experiences – especially in the "agreements" we make.[7] Satan will usually strategically wait until we are vulnerable – at a time when we are feeling hurt, betrayed, rejected, overlooked, etc. Then he suggests a lie to us - a false conclusion based on what we are experiencing. This is the critical moment. Will we agree with his suggestion or will we reject it? If we agree with Satan, a satanic lie becomes one of the many interrelated lies that weave together to create a false picture of reality in our minds– a way of seeing reality that will twist and warp our behavior based on what we believe is true. These lies are like cinder blocks in a wall – they are related to each other and support each other. Over time, these nests of interrelated false or partially false beliefs begin to seem self-evident in our thinking. We no longer even question whether or not they are true. We are fooled into thinking that behaviors based on these kinds of beliefs just have to be "right".

The ideas and thoughts we agree with that do not represent biblical truth are important because either the thoughts themselves are strongholds or lead us to believe things that are not true which then become strongholds. In other words, what we think determines what we believe – good or bad, right or wrong. Jesus said that we are what we believe. Our thoughts are simply unspoken words and the Bible makes it clear that we need to be very careful about how we use our words. Jesus said that we *speak* out of what is in our heart[8] (our in-most being) and that out of the heart come evil thoughts…that these thoughts are what pollutes us.[9] He also said that we will have to give account of every idle *word* we *speak*.[10] We are told that, if we confess with our *mouth* that Jesus is Lord, and believe in our heart that God raised him from the dead, we will be saved. The apostle Paul said, "…it is with our heart that we believe and are justified, and it is with our *mouth* that we confess and are saved."[11] We are also told that death and life are in the power of the *tongue*.[12] We know, of course, that the tongue itself is not the problem but the thoughts that are behind the *words* we *speak using our tongue*. Much of the third chapter of the book of James in the New Testament focuses on the dangers of how we use our tongue. It is like a small spark that can start a forest fire…that it can set the whole course of our life on fire… that out of our *mouths* can come both praises for God and cursing…that this ought not to be.[13] We can tame our tongue by first taming our mind and our emotions - the place where our thoughts originate. We can tame our mind and emotions by immersing them in and adjusting them to the word of God. Someone has used a tube of toothpaste as an object lesson to teach us about words. Once the toothpaste is squeezed out, there is no way to put it back in the tube. Once you speak words – blessing or cursing – they are out! If they are words of cursing, the only thing you can do is clean them up the best you can. How can you do that? By being willing to say, "That didn't come out right" or "That's not how I meant that to sound." Then, say what you meant, or ought to have said was…[14].

God spoke creation into being by His words. We also can 'create' either for good or bad by what we speak. Yes, words and the thoughts behind our words are very important. Our enemies (Satan and his helpers) don't know for sure what lies we have chosen to believe until we speak them because they can't read our mind. The ability to know what Christians are thinking is reserved only for our own minds and the Holy Spirit who lives in us. Satan is quite happy to just let lies fester in our minds unspoken. Be assured, however, that we will *speak* the things we have chosen to believe out loud, sooner or later, even if we don't recognize where they come from. As soon as we speak them, Satan will then know for sure and what we have chosen to believe. Then he can use those spoken lies against us and more successfully tempt us to sin and establish footholds related to the specific area of sin involved.

Another way we 'make agreements' (i.e. establish strongholds) is by choosing to believe things that we repeatedly hear, think, or speak that are damaging, negative things about ourselves - for example, things like, "I'll never measure up; I have to over-achieve to be loved or accepted; I have to be perfect or I'll be rejected; I'm not worthy to receive anything from God; If others knew what I am really like, they would reject me; etc." This kind of thought or speaking is often referred to as a "word curse". Word curses are simply part of the nest of lies related to or supporting a basic or primary stronghold or they may be the stronghold itself. These word curses that we speak or that others have spoken against us need to be recognized, repented of, and replaced with the truth like any other stronghold. Sometimes, the whole nest of related lies will fall like a house of cards when a primary stronghold is replaced with the truth. But, any that remain will need to be dealt with just like any other stronghold. The Bible says that, it is with our heart that we believe and are justified and it is with our mouth that we confess and are saved.[15] We might paraphrase this same principle with regard to strongholds: when we believe a lie in our mind and sooner or later express it with our mouth, we establish a stronghold. Someone has said that all words act as seeds that are planted in the hearts of those listening, whether they are words that we speak to others, words that are spoken to us, or even thoughts that may have been planted in our mind by ourselves, others, or by Satan. Every 'seed-word' potentially has the power to reproduce – so, plant seeds of blessing, hope, and encouragement in your own life and in the lives of others, not seeds of blame, shame, unforgiveness, or anything else that is potentially damaging or hurtful.

We not only need to be aware of the consequences of the words we speak, but we also need to be careful that we don't take the truths we learn (like those about word curses) to extremes. This is an area of truth, for example, that can easily be overused or misused. There are churches that teach people that they must never say anything that is negative in any way (even if it is true). Sometimes this teaching is referred to as the "negative confession" teaching. For example, if someone asks me whether or not I still have a headache, this teaching says that I must not admit that I still have the headache because that would be a "negative confession". This example could be funny if it weren't true. Our enemy will lead us into any kind of error he can – even taking God's truth to extremes. Just be aware of this possibility and compare any potential overuse or misuse of Biblical truth with the full teaching of the Bible. If you are not sure what that is, ask your pastor or a wise, mature fellow Christian. You can also purchase a good, easy to use Bible software program like *Logos*[16]. Even the most basic version comes with several Bible versions, commentaries, and other references to help you learn what Bible scholars believe and teach about almost any subject. As you grow in knowledge of the truth, you will want to get Bible reference materials anyway. A software program like *Logos* will give you the most bang-for-your-buck.

Because thoughts are words that just haven't been spoken yet, we also need to be careful about the thoughts we allow ourselves to think. Everything we have said about words applies to our thoughts too. In the New Testament, the focus is primarily on what people think – not just on what they say or do. We are told to smash warped philosophies, tear down barriers erected against the truth of God, and fit every loose thought and emotion and impulse into the structure of a life shaped by Christ.[17] One of the reasons we want to replace ungodly strongholds with God's truth is so we can recognize when sinful thoughts and temptations enter our mind - thoughts contrary to what God wants us to be thinking about – thoughts rooted in anything that does not come from faith because the Bible tells us that anything that does not come from faith is sin.[18] Strongholds are established primarily by sinful thoughts we have chosen to agree with and believe whether they are spoken or not. Some of the things that are most damaging in our lives might never become visible behaviors or actually be spoken. Thought patterns such as unforgiveness, fear, bitterness, hatred, anxiety, guilt, shame, condemnation, depression, pride, and self-hatred are always related to strongholds. As these thoughts become habitual thought patterns, they will inevitably result in sinful speech and behaviors, and, inevitably, become footholds that result in bondage.

You might be thinking, "God wants me to not only control what I do but also what I think? Impossible!" Yes, it is impossible – if we are trying to do it using only our own resources. Remember from chapter three that trying to use our own resources to obey God is sin that keeps us from having access to the resources that God has provided for us. It sets us up for failure and attack by the spirits of guilt, shame, condemnation, self hatred, and who knows how many others. But, of course, we are not asked to control our behavior and thoughts on our own. We are being asked to cooperate with the Holy Spirit within us to do it through us. Our thought life can, and will be washed clean by thinking about and meditating in God's written Word, the Bible.[19] None of us can live the Christian life without God's resources. Successfully living the Christian life in God's power is not only possible but is amazing and joyful; full of meaning, security, significance, intimacy, and adventure.[20]

Strongholds – part 3 - RECOGNIZING OUR STRONGHOLDS
(Possible chapter title?)
(This section itself should probably be broken up into 2 or 3 chapters)

In chapter three we discussed the ways God communicates with us including His *rhema* words that reveal His truth to us and speak directly to those issues that we are aware of or most concerned about. God is more than willing to reveal His truth to us. But we need to be prepared to hear it, want to hear it, be passionately seeking to hear it. How can we be ready to recognize those areas of our lives that need to be corrected – those areas of our lives where, perhaps, we can't recognize truth because we have believed lies? One of the best ways we can prepare ourselves to 'hear' God as we attempt to recognize our strongholds is to spend some time thinking about and appreciating those times when He has spoken to us – the times when we felt we were in touch with God in a personal, interactive, contingent way. It is also helpful to journal about those times in as much detail as we can remember. As we do this, it makes it much easier to remember them. If you can't remember a time when you felt you were in touch with God in this way, then try to remember and appreciate a time when you have felt touched deeply by the beauty of nature or music or art. God 'speaks' to us in many ways. As we consciously, intentionally choose to recognize and thank Him for the good things we do experience in our lives, we will also grow in our abilities to 'hear' His *rhema* communications to us too.

We already know that the ultimate result of believing lies (establishing satanic strongholds in our lives) is bondage to satanic influence in those areas of our lives. We also know that these beliefs are usually in blind spots – ways of thinking that we don't even realize exist. So, what are the clues that will help us become concerned about the things God wants to show us? When Jesus taught, He often asked questions that helped direct people's thinking. When we are willing to seriously and honestly ask the right questions about what is going on in our lives, we will begin to see the results of the bondage that we are in. We will begin to be concerned about the source of those consequences. It is at this point that God can begin to reveal truth to us about both the lies we have believed and the truth that He wants those lies to be replaced with. Long-term freedom from bondage is only possible when we tear down strongholds and replace them with the Godly beliefs, the truth He has revealed to us. When Godly beliefs are established, Satan will still try to get us to believe his lies, but we will be less likely to be deceived because the truth has already been intentionally and firmly established at that point. After we do that, we are then able to consciously reject any thought that does not conform to the truth. Of course, sometimes that is more easily said than done because of the habitual thought processes we have established before replacing the lie with truth. We'll talk more about that later.

I have listed some questions later in this chapter that you can ask yourself to help you recognize things that you might need to be concerned about. Once you've begun to identify some of these things, you can then begin to ask yourself and God some follow-up questions like: "What do I really believe about this? When did I first begin to believe this? Is there a painful experience related to this? Is what I believe really the truth according to what Scripture teaches? Jesus, what is this all about? What do you want me to see?" As you consider these questions, consciously, intentionally open yourself up to the revelation of truth (rhema) from God (not just the reasoning of your own intellect). Real truth, real understanding, real insight into what you actually believe will come only as God directs your reasoning and thinking. To be truly effective and lasting, this whole process needs to be one that God directs and that we simply cooperate with. Answering these questions will almost always also reveal the footholds (areas of sin) we are dealing with in our lives – and, often, the strongholds too. Deal with the footholds you discover as you become aware of them. This will limit Satan's ability to control, influence, or interfere as you deal with the stronghold that allowed the foothold(s) to be established in the first place. You have already learned about how to deal with footholds in chapter four.

I want to encourage you again to begin journaling your thoughts and questions about each area of concern you are working on at the moment. Based on my own experience and that of countless others, you might find yourself processing more than one area of concern over a period of several weeks. God seems to reveal things to me slowly over a period of time (sometimes from a wide range of sources) – just enough to take me to the next level of understanding about what He wants me to see. Keep pursuing the same area(s) of insight until you have a clear picture of the lie(s) you believed and what the truth really is. The truth revealed will be, in one way or another, the opposite of the lie. Or, the lie(s) revealed will be the opposite of the truth, depending upon which is revealed first.

When you journal, you record this process so you don't lose key ideas, or questions, or understandings. Record whatever comes to your mind – whatever you become aware of whether or not it seems important at that moment. Once you have recorded them, you can go back over them later and evaluate them. Ask Jesus to highlight in your awareness which thoughts He wants to talk to you about. As the process continues, link each subsequent journal entry for a particular area of concern to the next (and vice-versa) so you can keep all your associated journal entries connected. When I re-read my journal entries about a particular area of concern at a later time (so that I can see the whole process with 20-20 hindsight), I feel so grateful that it didn't get dumped on me all at once. So often, the impact of the insights and understandings might have been just too overwhelming and sometimes painful too - tempting me to back away from the whole process. Also, with 20-20 hindsight, I'm so glad that I didn't get overwhelmed and back away. C. S. Lewis must have experienced these same feelings because, in one of his letters to a friend, he wrote,

> "I sometimes pray, 'Lord give me *no more* and *no less* self-knowledge than I can at this moment make good use of.' Remember, He is the artist and you are only the picture. You can't see it. So, quietly submit to being painted...."[21]

When we discover and actually recognize the lies we have believed about God, ourselves, or others and realize the consequences in our life from them, we almost surely will be tempted to entertain thoughts of guilt, shame, self-loathing- self-hatred, self-condemnation, and unforgiveness of ourselves. Don't buy into any of this! The truth is that only those who are really focusing on walking with God and seeking the truth will recognize the terrible godlessness of these lies and the sin that results from them. Use these insights as a reminder to forgive yourself and confess any known sin associated with cooperating with Satan and believing his lies. Then, move on with the process of getting free. Don't allow yourself to get stuck at this point in the process. Satan would like nothing better than to have us get stuck in fear, guilt, shame, or self-condemnation as we begin to recognize the extent of our own sinfulness. If you are feeling stuck, take a break and intentionally focus on and appreciate the good times you have had in God's presence. This will take you to a safe place in your thinking and help get you unstuck.

Also, don't be fearful that God will reveal a stronghold or a memory to you that will be too much for you to handle. The Bible uses two different words for 'time' – one is for chronological or progressive time and the other is for strategic time. You can always trust that God's timing in showing you what you need to deal with is always strategically perfect. God will progressively reveal the truth we need only when we need it and only when we are ready for it.

I have included several examples of my own stronghold-related journaling process in Appendix B. Including these very personal thoughts makes me feel 'exposed' for all to see. But, it will be well worth my feeling a little discomfort if you find them instructive and valuable as you embark on your own journaling process.

As we begin to look for strongholds, there will be periods when we don't seem to be getting any new or fresh insights. At these times we will be tempted to feel anxious, like nothing important is happening, like we have hit some kind of a road block. When we're feeling blocked, we need to consciously, intentionally relax and recall those times when we felt we were receiving and appreciating new and fresh insights from God. Going back to our memories of these successful, fruitful connections with God give us a safe place to return to. We can then (when we are ready to start again) ask God to help us see whatever might be blocking our progress in getting free from the footholds, strongholds, or toxic memories that seem to be blocking our sense of closeness with Him. This is a process that can't be hurried.

Many of us have been raised with a belief that God is angry and mean - just waiting for us to mess up so he can judge and punish us.

This belief itself is a stronghold and can block us from admitting that we might have any beliefs that could cause God to judge and reject us. Others might judge or reject us because of our beliefs, but God never will. On the contrary, He is at the very center of this whole process of helping us discover strongholds and truth so we can be free and experience His unlimited, amazing, unconditional love for us. God values our openness and searching for truth because His very nature is the essence of absolute truth.

Sometimes, trying too hard can itself be the cause of blockage. When we are feeling blocked, we need to be especially careful to avoid what has been called 'morbid introspection'. If we are looking and looking to find something wrong, we will probably find something to obsess about (like any good hypochondriac). If we are simply open to allowing the Lord to help us recognize anything He wants us to take a look at and correct (with His help and in His timing), we are in no danger of getting ourselves into trouble. So, before we begin to look for strongholds that we are not already aware of, we need to take a moment to pray something like this:

> *"Jesus, you know what needs to be worked on next. Will you please guide my thinking in this process? Please keep me from 'finding' things that aren't real or that I'm not ready to deal with yet. Lord, I want to take this journey into self-knowledge only at your pace and only as you guide this process."*

John Eldredge reveals his approach to praying for guidance – how he asks God for insight into the things God wants to show him:

> *"Oh Holy Spirit, you have come to lead me into all truth, to reveal to me the things of God (John 16:12–15). You reveal deep and hidden things; you know what lies in darkness, and light dwells within you (Daniel 2:22). Awaken me morning by morning; awaken my ear like one being taught (Isaiah 50:4). Reveal to me what you are speaking through the events in my life. Enable me to hear and understand your voice more clearly. I ask in Jesus name."*[22]

It might seem like the process of searching for the lies we have believed and learning the truth is like fishing. Gerald May describes it pretty well:

"You cast your line into the dark, unseen, depths and something is alive there, and it connects, and you start to bring it to the surface, to daylight, to consciousness, and you begin to wonder if you really want to see what it is. But there it is whatever it is, on the end of your line. Like it or not, you are connected. Committed. Enchanted."[23]

Our behavior (good or bad) is based on what we *really* believe is true - not what we think we ought to believe or even what we *think* we believe at a surface level. When the things we truly believe don't represent truth, our thoughts and behaviors get us into trouble. When these true beliefs are in blind spots as they almost always are, we need some help to discover them. We know enough about strongholds now to see them for what they are if we can just get some good clues to get our thinking and God's revelation processes started. One way to get this kind of help is to consider questions that will give us clues. So, here are a few questions that can help facilitate our discovery process:

- What wrong behaviors or sins am I struggling with?

  We already know that, when we choose to sin, a foothold (a place of bondage to a particular sin or an area of sin) is established.[24] A devotional book I was reading last year provided the following insight:

  When you are plagued by a persistent sin problem – one that goes on and on, view it is a rich opportunity. An ongoing problem is like a tutor who always is by your side. The learning possibilities are limited only by your willingness to be teachable. In faith, thank Jesus for your problem. Ask him to open your eyes and your heart to all that he is accomplishing through this difficulty. Once you have become grateful for a problem, it loses its power to drag you down. On the contrary, you're thankful attitude will lift you up into heavenly places with Jesus. From this perspective, your difficulty can seem as a slight, temporary, distress that is producing for you a transcendent glory never to cease![25]

  Jesus said we can know a tree by its fruit.[26] We can also know the source of a thought or belief by its fruit. Does it produce faith and the fruit of the Spirit[27] or does it produce the fruit of sin[28]? If the result is sin, your belief is a stronghold or related to a stronghold.

The sin that we recognize and struggle with can give us the clues we need to begin thinking more clearly about, "What do I really believe about this area of behavior in my life?" For example, if I'm struggling with anger, it is almost always because I think someone is somehow blocking me from getting what I want. Ask Jesus, "Lord, where is this coming from? What is this about? What do I really believe about my right to get what I want when I want it? Why do I allow myself to behave angrily toward others? When was the first time I remember experiencing this kind of anger?" Remembering the first time we felt or reacted in a particular way can also lead us to a toxic memory that Jesus wants to heal. The answers to these kinds of questions can be as varied as the number of people who ask them. Write down both the questions and the responses or impressions you 'hear' in your journal and review them periodically. Often, the initial impressions I get as I continue this process leads me to ask more pointed questions until I finally have a fairly clear picture of what I have believed that is not true. I can then ask God to show me what the truth is that He wants used to replace the lie. The truth will be the opposite of the lie and will always be in agreement with what the Bible has to say. If I recognize the truth first, then I can use it to lead me to the lie which, in one way or another, will be the opposite of or deny the truth. This is the general process you can use with each of these questions. If you are having problems answering this question, and, you feel really brave, and, you feel that you also have really strong ego strength, ask your spouse what they would answer if they were answering for you. This will also helpful to give you insight for any of the questions below. We will discuss the actual process of replacing the lie with the truth in more detail in the last section of this chapter. If you come up empty as you consider a question, move on to the next – or take a break and allow a little time for an insight to surface. This is a process that takes time. Don't try to rush it.

- What are the desires I have that might get me into trouble?

Most of us look at our desires and try to repress them so they don't get out of control. The Bible says,

"Something has gone wrong deep within me and gets the better of me every time. It happens so regularly that it's predictable. The moment I decide to do good, sin is there to trip me up. I truly delight in God's commands, but it's pretty obvious that not all of me joins in that delight. Parts of me covertly rebel, and just when I least expect it, they take charge."[29]

"For the sinful nature desires what is contrary to the spirit and the spirit desires what is contrary to the sinful nature. They are in conflict with each other, so that you do not do what you want."[30]

How we go about fulfilling our desires is a key to recognizing our strongholds. Eldredge says it this way:

There is a nagging awareness inside us, warning that we better not feel our hunger to deeply or it will undo us. We might do something crazed, desperate. We are caught on the horns of the dilemma; our unmet desires are a source of trouble, and it feels as if it will get worse if we allow ourselves to feel how much we do desire. Not only that, we often don't know what we desire....Our dilemma is this: we can't seem to live with desire, and we can't live without it. In the face of this quandary, most people decide to bury the whole question and put as much distance as they can between themselves and their desires. It is a logical and tragic act. The tragedy is increased tenfold when this suicide of soul is committed under the conviction that this is precisely what Christianity recommends. We have never been more mistaken.... it's not that the longing roused by any of these things is wrong.[31]

We need to recognize and acknowledge the desires that we are feeling and ask ourselves what is behind them, "Is what am I believing potentially 'setting me up' to allow a desire to get out of control?" When we focus on and fear our desires, we are focusing on a symptom – not a cause. It is very dangerous to treat symptoms and not correct causes! When we focus on sinful desires rather than the stronghold behind them, we are focusing on symptoms rather than causes. What beliefs are behind our evil desires - justifying our sinful behaviors and getting us progressively further into bondage through footholds? We need to get rid of footholds when we recognize them – but, sooner or later, we will re-establish them if we don't deal with the reason we keep establishing them. Focusing on desires is what leads us to get addicted to counterfeit, substitute satisfactions rather than the only true source of satisfaction – God himself. C. S. Lewis put it this way:

Indeed…our Lord finds our desires not too strong, but too weak. We are half–hearted creatures, fooling around with drink and sex and ambition when infinite joy is offered us, like an ignorant child who wants to go on making mud pies in a slum because he cannot imagine what is meant by the offer of a holiday at the sea. We are far too easily pleased…. The [substitutes] in which we thought [satisfaction] was located will betray us if we trust to them; it was not *in* them, it only came *through* them, and what came through them was longing. These things – the [substitutes we have pursued in] our own past – are good images of what we really desire; but if they are mistaken for the real thing itself, they turn into dumb idols, breaking the hearts of their worshipers. For they are not the thing itself; they are only the scent of a flower we have not found, the echo of a tune we have not heard, news from a country we have not yet visited….If a transtemporal, transfinite good is our real destiny, then any other good on which our desire fixes must be in some degree fallacious, must bear at best only a symbolical relation to what will truly satisfy.[32] (word substitutions in brackets - are mine to more closely reflect the language used in this book)

We can get good clues to recognize our strongholds when we discover we are seeking to satisfy our true needs, wants, or desires with substitutes. Dan Allender has observed:

The heart cannot help but hope, but it is reluctant to let hope press unrestrained toward its fulfillment – heaven. Instead, we live out our desire … in pursuing good times, good sex, a new car, a steady boyfriend, a few weeks of rest from labor. All these desires are legitimate. The problem is that few see them in the light of what each ultimately inches toward. Each has the power to delight and please, but will lose its meaning unless it is seen in the light of deeper anticipation.[33]

How can we deal with our tendency to seek out these substitutes? Allender goes on to say:

The answer, in part, is to enter deeply into our hunger for more and the disappointment of incompleteness. Hunger and disappointment serve as internal witnesses against all efforts to make any part of our existence into a real piece of heaven. Our tendency is to satisfy our desire... in some activity as mundane as keeping the car clean, the Day-Timer organized, and the grass green. Nothing is wrong with these activities, as long as each continually frustrates us with a failure that edges us beyond the mundane to something so mysterious and wonderful that all frustration, failure, and struggle is light, momentary affliction in comparison.[34]

Most of our "desires" are rooted in a God–given hunger to find the beauty and perfection of a complete, unhindered, restored, reconciled relationship with God – to experience the reality of our future in heaven – not the substitutes we all so easily settle for. Eldredge observes that, the more attuned we are to our true desires, the less prone we'll be to accept the substitutes.[35] If this brief discussion about desire and the substitutes we use to satisfy them strikes a chord in you, I recommend that you read Eldredge's book, *The Journey of Desire* and, perhaps also, work through the companion journal and guidebook.

In one of his workbooks, Eldredge asked a very interesting and revealing question: How do the "Godly" people in your church handle desire?[36] It seems to me that most people I know, including myself, often push desire away because it can result in sinful excesses or profound disappointment. It is true, far too often, when we embrace desire, the process is tainted by self-effort or self-fulfillment. When we're successful in fulfilling our desire, we get a measure of satisfaction and don't realize that we are embracing substitutes for the reality and true satisfaction that God wants to provide. For a long time, I held desire at arm's length and then went about fulfilling it by my own efforts. Even though our desires can be 'dangerous' if they are given free-reign, at its core, Christianity motivates us by inviting us to '*desire*'.[37]

- What am I over-reacting to or reacting inappropriately to?

    When we recognize that we have reacted in a way that is out of proportion to what triggered it, we have stumbled into a clue that there is something else going on – some belief in a blind spot that we are actually reacting to. For example, I some time ago, I realized that I was over reacting to a dog that refused to be house trained and, also, (within myself) to a person who was refusing to cooperate with *my* efforts to help them. I realized that these responses were somehow related to a stronghold I had not yet identified and dealt with (or that I had only partially dealt with). I felt that it had something to do with a need to control. I've summarized some of my own journaling process to deal with this in Appendix B.

- What do I believe or what are my assumptions about it being God's job to give me a happy, successful, joyful, life?

    Eldredge notes that one of our most common, most unquestioned, and most naïve assumptions is that 'it is God's job to give me a happy life and shield me from most problems'. He says,

    We assume that because we believe in God, and because he is love, he's going to give us a happy life. A + B = C. You may not be so bold as to state this assumption out loud – you may not even think you hold this assumption – but notice your shock when things don't go well. Notice your feelings of abandonment and betrayal when life doesn't work out. Notice that often you feel as though God isn't really all that close, or involved, feel that he isn't paying attention to your life.... Our assumptions control our interpretation of events, and they supply a great deal of momentum and direction for our lives. It's important that we look at them. And life will provide hundreds of opportunities to take a look at our assumptions in a single week. Especially when we walk with God....*We* seek for life and look to God as *our* assistant in the endeavor.....[38]

I once heard a pastor use an illustration. He said that, if you place a flea in a jar and put a lid on the jar, the flea will try to jump out of the jar – which it could easily do if the lid wasn't there. The flea tries to jump out repeatedly but bumps into the lid. It soon learns that, when it jumps, it hits the lid and it quits trying to jump. You can then take the lid off the jar and the flea will remain trapped. I have forgotten what the point of his illustration was but I haven't forgotten the illustration. We are all like the flea. We assume that something is true so we stop even questioning whether it is true or not. The things we assume are true when they really are not true *are* our strongholds in which we are trapped. Unfortunately, we usually act on them and get ourselves trapped even further.

I had a stronghold in the past that went something like this, "If it is to be it is up to me." I think I picked this idea up from a textbook or perhaps at a motivational seminar. Whatever the source, I made an agreement with it. I occasionally even quoted it proudly. This stronghold then evolved into, "If God doesn't meet my needs or wants, then, it is up to me to do it for myself." In the context of 'It is up to God to give me a happy life', it doesn't take much imagination to figure out how much trouble this particular stronghold could and did get me into.

When we realize that we have bought into the idea that it is God's job to assure us a happy life, then, we need to ask ourselves other questions: What are the things in my life, or in my desires, or in my dreams that I think would make me happy *without* God? What do I desire? Why do I desire these things? What thought or idea have I agreed with that would allow me to have the things or relationships I want *now* apart from God to give me happiness, joy, acceptance, approval, love, recognition, someone who cares enough to listen, security, accomplishment, fulfillment, etc....(You fill in the blank)...? We all want these things in our lives and, for the most part, should. But, these are the things that can become our addictions, our substitutes, our idols if we allow them to. How do we go about getting what we want?

I know a Christian woman who is not experiencing the things she wants and she is feeling depressed. Her depression is leading her towards food as one of her substitutes for joy, acceptance, and whatever else it is that she wants in her life. It is true that our substitutes do make us feel better in the very short term – but, like all addictions, more and more of our 'drug of choice' is needed to make us feel better. One of her drugs of choice is food. As her weight gets further and further out of control, she is not getting the love and acceptance she wants from her husband. Instead she is getting the opposite – criticism, disrespect, and rejection. The heavier she gets, the more depressed, needy, and physically sick she gets. The more her husband and others reject her, the more the cycle continues and deepens. She is making agreements – strongholds along the lines of, "My husband doesn't love me – maybe he never did", "I will never be truly loved.", "Love never stays." (she has experienced divorce more than once already). Of course, her husband has his own set of strongholds that are influencing his wrong behavior towards her. How can we get out of this kind of downward spiral? We need to recognize that we are trying to get happiness and joy from substitutes that can never give us what we truly want in the long term. We need to ask God to show us the lies we have believed and what His truth really is. Recognize that our sense of desire and misery is being used by the enemy to offer us lies about what will make us happy; and that it is *not* up to us to arrange for a happy life by our own efforts. True happiness will only come as God helps us to get rid of our substitutes and walk with Him in freedom and true fulfillment.

- What do I privately fear that God might take away?

This question is strongly related to the one above but it comes at it from a different direction. Of course, there are very few things in this life that cannot be lost. But, the question is pointing to what God might need to thwart to get our attention. Eldredge says it this way:

And so God must, from time to time, and sometimes very insistently, disrupt our lives *so that* we will release our grasping of life here and now….God is asking us to let go of the things we love, and have given our hearts to, so that we can give our hearts even more fully to him. He thwarts us in our attempts to make life work, so that our efforts fail, and we must face the fact that we really don't look to God for life. Our first reaction is usually to get angry with him, which only serves to make the point. Don't you hear people say, "Why did God let this happen?" far more than you hear them say, "Why aren't I more fully given over to God?" Far too often, we see God as a means to an end rather than the end in itself - God as the assistant to *our* life versus God as our life.[39]

Answering this question can give us a good clue to what we believe might be more important to us than God- what our idols (and our substitutes) are. Some people fear that something bad will happen to them because they are not perfect – because they sin. This is a stronghold that is actually taught by some churches. It goes something like this, "God is watching you and just waiting for you to make some kind of misstep or sin so that he can punish you." If you have had thoughts like this or actually been taught that this is what God is like, then here is a possible truth statement for you: "If something is taken away or thwarted by God, it is because of his love for me - to redirect my focus to him and bring me greater blessing and spiritual growth." There is an infinitely big difference between God's punishment and God's loving discipline. The Bible says that if we will judge ourselves we won't need to be disciplined.[40]

- What kinds of things or activities am I strongly drawn to that I know are not 'right' or healthy for me?

Take a look at your pleasures and distractions: food, sleep, work, books, hobbies, TV, movies, sexually oriented stuff, anything done or used to an excess. These things don't have to be things we would normally recognize as sin. What is their function? Are they substitutes for the way God wants to meet those needs? What beliefs are hiding behind our involvement with these things? Our pleasures and distractions can also be clues to the thoughts we may have made agreements with. I want to remind you of an earlier word of caution. As you consider these questions, don't get drawn into 'morbid introspection'. If the enemy of your soul can't trip you up one way, he'll try another. Be on your guard but not paranoid as you consider these ideas.

- What recurring dreams do you have?

The Bible has many stories about people who were guided by or warned by dreams. The three wise men who visited the baby Jesus were warned in a dream not to go back home through Jerusalem.[41] Joseph (the Virgin Mary's husband) was told in a dream to take Mary and Jesus down to Egypt for a while.[42] Someone has said that, "Our dreams are just a safe way for us to go a little crazy safely." I agree with that to some degree. I think that most of our dreams probably fall into that category. There are some dreams, however, that we should give at least a second look. I was reminded of a recurring dream that I had had on and off over a period of several years. Because I was aware that strongholds are often in blind spots and that dreams can be used by God to make us aware of things we might need to take a look at, I asked God to show me if this recurring dream was one of those. In my very vivid series of dreams, I found myself in various settings hiding behind things or running from one place of cover to another because, although I was fully dressed otherwise, I was naked from the waist down in my dream. I discovered that this dream was related to the nest of strongholds that "I had to over-achieve to be loved and accepted – that, otherwise, I didn't 'measure up' and I would be discovered for what I 'really' was." If, for some reason, I couldn't overachieve, then I would do my best to cover it up in one way or another (hide behind whatever was available). After the Lord dealt with this nest of related strongholds and showed me the related truths, these particular dreams stopped completely. Coincidence? Maybe. But, I don't think so.

- What kinds of things start my thoughts down paths that I don't (or perhaps shouldn't) want them to go to?

These kinds of thoughts might be negative things am I saying to myself on a regular basis (word curses). What do I believe about myself that is negative? What have others said about me that is negative that I agree with? We have had much to say above about these issues and about the need for self-forgiveness. When we repeat a lie over and over again in our mind, we begin to believe it. The reason we want to ask these questions in this context is to give us the clues we need to deal with the lies that we believe about ourselves. I can't think of an instance when negative self-talk isn't rooted, in one way or another, in a nest of strongholds. Very often, these thoughts are strongholds themselves.

Another category of thoughts related to this question is daydreams and fantasies. Daydreams and fantasies have a lot to do with what kind of material we are exposing ourselves to (romance novels, books, movies, TV programs, internet related stuff, etc. When we expose ourselves to material with explicitly negative, violent, sexual, or otherwise inappropriate content, we usually find our minds drifting into daydreams and fantasies about those things. The first thing we need to do, of course, is to take those thoughts captive and eject them from our minds.[43] The second thing we need to do immediately is to ask the Lord to show us what is going on in our belief systems that allow us to intentionally expose ourselves to that kind of material. The third thing to do is to stop exposing ourselves to that kind of stuff because it can come back to 'haunt' us later in life. It is not uncommon for me to have to 'take captive' and reject thoughts stirred up from stuff I exposed myself to a very long time ago. Exposing ourselves to things that are wrong, or even sometimes just to things that are 'questionable', often has to do with trying to make ourselves happy by choosing substitute pleasures. Once again, don't let Satan tempt you to take these ideas to extremes. If you have questions about something, just ask God to show you the truth. The Bible says He wants "everyone to be saved and to understand the truth".[44]

- What is going "wrong" in your life right now?

Other questions related to this include: What do my problems reveal about what I really believe? What is God up to by allowing this in my life? Eldredge observes:

Both dragons [big problems in our life] and nits [smaller problems in our life] take us into the places in the soul, uncovering the sentences we have long lived by. It was in the depths of his personal tragedies that Job uttered the ruling sentence of his heart: "What I had feared has come upon me." In other words, "I knew it! I knew I could not really trust God – not with things that really matter most." Job's idol was control and God was determined to save him from it. When the nits and dragons come, we ask God to remove them, and when He doesn't. We take charge of our own well-being, since it appears no one else will. The dragons and the nits reveal to us ... where our attachments and addictions lie. In other words, they reveal where our heart is, other than captured by the love of God.[45]

Too often, we are unable or unwilling to recognize the things God wants to show us through the problems in our lives. When things go wrong, our true beliefs often bubble to the fringe of our consciousness where we can become vaguely aware of them. Sometimes, we just push them back down and refuse to even consider them in the context of, "What is God up to in this?" I have a very personal example of how God uses things in our lives to grow us. Several years ago my wife was diagnosed with an illness called Primary Progressive Aphasia. It is a rare form of dementia that is progressively affecting her ability to speak, understand instructions, reason, and make decisions. There is currently no effective medical cure or treatment for it. We are praying for healing and, at the same time dealing with the reality of the disease. For us, this is a "dragon". God has revealed several things in both my wife and me through this illness which has given us the opportunity to grow both spiritually and in our relationship with Him and each other. I sense there is even more that He wants us to 'see' if this disease continues to progress.

- What sort of Freudian slips do I make?

  Be aware that so-called "Freudian slips" can alert us to things we believe whether or not we consciously think we do. Therapists recognize that these slips of the tongue are often statements of truth (positive or negative) coming from the unconscious part of the mind.[46] When this happens to us, we need to stop for a moment and ask questions, "What was 'that' all about? Jesus, is there anything there that I need to be aware of and deal with?" Sometimes we can get further clues by looking at what it was that triggered whatever 'slipped out'.

- What sort of offenses have I experienced lately? What do I take offense at? What am I grumbling or complaining about?

  The kinds of things we get easily upset about can give us clues about traumatic things we have experienced in the past. Perhaps we agreed with a thought or made a vow not to allow that to happen to us again. Whenever something like that happens to us again, it triggers strong emotions. For example, when I'm stopped in traffic because lanes are closed ahead and someone comes zipping by so they can cut-in way ahead, I have a strong, negative reaction. I still don't know what that is all about but, someday, I'll figure it out and deal with it. Till then, my poor wife puts up with my grumbling comments. Even if I don't say anything, she knows what is going on inside me. At some point in my life, I allowed an experience to generate a belief, which resulted in a stronghold, which will result in a foothold (bondage) if I allow these kinds of thoughts. I might also be tempted to do something really stupid and act on them.

- Why am I doing what I am doing in the way I am doing it?

    Another way of asking this question is: What are my motives?[47] Out of our true beliefs (godly or not godly), we develop reasons for doing what we do the way we do it. This is why Jesus stressed the importance of our motives. Depending upon our motive, a specific behavior is sin or it isn't.[48] When we choose to sin, a foothold is established.[49] When we look at our motives honestly, we will discover that some motives seem good and some are not as good as they ought to be. Sometimes, looking at our motives (especially the "not-so-good ones") or any of the things that these questions lead us to think about makes it easier to discover the true belief behind the motive. So, once we have the idea of what our motive is, then we can more successfully take the next step of discovery: *"Jesus, please show me the lies I have believed behind these wrong motives."* Eldredge observes that we need to be willing to hear *anything* God wants to say.[50] Otherwise, we are not likely to hear anything at all.

- What new truth has jumped out at you recently?

    Often, as we read the Bible or, perhaps, a book written by someone we know to be trustworthy, we begin to understand a "new" truth we hadn't previously seen. These times present us with a rare opportunity to shed light on blind spots. As God reveals new truth to us, we can consider it and ask ourselves whether or not it conflicts with or contradicts anything we have previously thought was as true. If it does, we may have discovered a potential stronghold that we weren't previously aware of. If we determine that it is one, we can pull it down and replace it with God's truth.

- What "vows" (commitments) have you made as a result of experiences in your life?

    I know a lady who had an angry and controlling alcoholic father. As an adult, she entered into several relationships that were also controlling and abusive. Somewhere along the way (probably as a child) she made a subconscious vow that, "I will never allow anyone to control me like that again" - even though she continued entering into abusive relationships after she became an adult. Whenever she thought that someone was trying to control her, she became angry and aggressively attacked the "controlling" person verbally and, sometimes, physically. Her responses came from hidden places in her mind. They "felt" like reasonable reactions to her 'present' circumstances – but they were not. She had become an abuser herself and used anger to try to control the situation she found herself in. She also became an alcoholic herself trying to deal with the on-going unhappiness of her life. Although she didn't know it at the time, she had given a foothold to spirits of anger, abuse, and control. She established a stronghold when she made that vow and the destructive events in her life naturally followed. The truth she discovered is slowly but surely setting her free.

There are many other questions we could ask ourselves to give us clues about our strongholds. I think you have the idea now how this works. So, I'll just list a few other questions that have occurred to me without explanation or comment. If one jumps out at you as important for you, then ask God to help you see what He wants to reveal to you with regard to that question.

- Are you too connected emotionally to others in a way that could lead you into inappropriate relationships?

- Have you been tempted to separate yourself from others or even from God?[51]

- What are you trying to 'control' in your life?

- In what ways have you been "seduced" by Satan or his helpers into trying to live life on your own terms?

- What desires have you had recently that you felt were stupid, bad, or embarrassing?

- What kinds of things have you said to yourself recently (your "self–talk") when you have failed, felt regret, or had disappointments?

- What do you think Jesus feels about you? ...do you see how this might be connected to your brokenness? Is this how everyone else feels about you? How do you feel about yourself? Ask the Holy

Spirit – the Spirit of Truth – to show you how this is connected to your brokenness [strongholds].[52]

There may be other questions I haven't listed that might be unique to you or your situation. What other questions does God want you to ask yourself? There is an excellent book by Larry Osborne titled *10 dumb Things Smart Christians Believe* that is be a good source of additional questions to think about. If you have believed any of these 'dumb things', ask yourself, "What kind of sinful behavior (bondage) does believing these things set me up for?" This book includes an excellent basis for coming up with Biblical truth statements to replace these beliefs with. I've referenced this book in Appendix A in the Biblical Truth and Discipleship section.

In the context of talking about getting caught up in world events like war, the problems of work, or other distractions, C. S. Lewis made a suggestion that is very helpful for all of us:

> If we let ourselves, we shall always be waiting for some other distraction or other to end before we can get down to our work. The only people who achieve much are those who want knowledge so badly that they will seek it while the conditions are still unfavorable. Favorable conditions never come. There are, of course, moments when the pressure of the excitement is so great that only superhuman self-control could resist it. They come both in war and peace. We must do the best we can… A more Christian attitude, which can be attained at any age, is that of leaving futurity in God's hands. We may as well, for God will certainly retain it whether we leave it to him or not. Never in peace or war, commit your virtue or your happiness to the future. Happy work is best done by the man who takes his long-term plans somewhat lightly and works from moment to moment "as to the Lord." It is only our *daily* bread that we are encouraged to ask for. The present is the only time in which any duty can be done, or any grace received.[53]

Satan doesn't want you to discover the nests of lies he has so carefully hidden in your blind spots. He will try to get you to focus on anything else that might keep you from looking for and recognizing the strongholds in your life. Stick with this process for the rest of your life. Don't allow yourself to get side-tracked by anything – not politics, not the current economy, not better circumstances, not anything.

As we consider these questions and are open for God to show us what He wants us to recognize, Satan, or our own rational process, may suggest that the 'impressions' we receive are just the result of our own intellectual work, thinking, puzzling, or imagination. Of course, this is possible. Own biases and preferences whether right or wrong, including the inclinations of our own sin nature and self-interest, do have an influence in establishing what we think is true. So, how do we know when we are hearing revelation from God or misdirection from Satan or our own imagination? Because we do live in a war zone and we do have an enemy, we always need to check all 'spiritual insights' or 'revelations' against Biblical truth. The Bible tells us to evaluate "revelations and prophesies to see if they are true.[54] One of the gifts of the Holy Spirit is the "discernment of spirits".[55] We each have this ability to some degree. If you have any doubts, seek out other Christians whose maturity and wisdom you know you can trust to help you evaluate your 'revelation'. With time and experience you will discover how well you can trust your ability to discern the sources of your 'insights'. Also, I have personally observed that, as I ponder whether or not something is true, discuss it with others, and check it against Biblical truth, God will use even the intentionally deceptive suggestions of Satan, others, and my own self-interest to reveal truth to me that I might not otherwise have recognized. God will do this for you too. So, don't be afraid of this process simply because it is possible that you could be temporarily misled. Continue your growth process confidently and trust the Holy Spirit within you (God) to protect you and reveal His truth to you. You can count on this happening because one of the Holy Spirit's jobs is to reveal truth to us.[56]

Here are some of the things I've 'heard' as I considered these questions:

> "Stop looking for strongholds in your life. You are becoming an extremist - seeing demonic attack all around – don't get carried away."

> "You are who you are. Don't be concerned about strongholds."

> "There is no hope that you will ever become the man of God you think you want to be. Who do you think you are?"

"If anything is going to happen, you will have to do it yourself. That is what all this stuff about strongholds really is anyway – just your imagination." This is a variation on an old stronghold that I've had to tear down more than once, "I can't trust God to meet my needs – I'll have to do it myself."

If I agree with any of these thoughts, then I will have begun to re-establish or add to strongholds that I'll just have to tear down again later. Just reject thoughts like these to start with 'in Jesus' name' (using His delegated authority- not yours). Also, when I think these kinds of thoughts, I'm reminded of something Eldredge wrote:

> It is so hard at these times to sort out what is going on. What is genuine conviction, and what is assault? What is my fault and what is warfare? And where is the warfare coming from? Start with this – you shall know them by their fruits. Genuine conviction brings repentance. But not judgment, not contempt. Genuine conviction brings us back to God. It doesn't say to us, *you've blown it so bad, he's removed himself from you.* I have to start with the fruit of this…. I feel far from God. This is not from the Holy Spirit. Right now, that's all of about all I know.[57]

Each of us has a personality that is different from others. We each also have a wonderful set of strengths associated our personalities. When we overuse or misuse our strengths, they become our 'weaknesses'; and, we all overuse or misuse our strengths more than we realize. When we overuse or misuse our strengths, we are sinning because doing anything apart from faith is sin[58] and, when we sin, we establish footholds. Because of the strengths and weaknesses we all have, we are also predisposed to certain motivations and ways of seeing the world. In other words, the natural tendencies associated with our personalities predispose us to certain kinds of strongholds. Satan and his helpers understand our natural tendencies and will try to use them against us. That is another reason we all need to be aware of and use this process of dealing with the strongholds and footholds in our lives. If you would like to learn more about personalities, refer to Appendix A.

EXAMPLES OF STRONGHOLDS
(This is another possible chapter title.)

We have provided many examples of strongholds throughout this book already. God can also reveal strongholds to us through a list of typical, common strongholds. I have included a list of typical strongholds (Ungodly Beliefs) taken, in part, from an excellent book on healing and deliverance[59] in Appendix C. As you read through them, seeking revelation from God. You might recognize several things that you have believed.

In Chapter two, I described my first experience of recognizing a stronghold. The stronghold I had believed was, "There is no such thing as unconditional love – even God's." This was reinforced by the fact that God had established a lot of rules - lots of *dos and don'ts*; which (as I misinterpreted it) meant that, "It was up to me to earn God's love by obeying all the rules." This belief, supported by the behavior of my parents, then led me to believe that, "I have to earn others love and approval through over-achievement." Later in life, I made an agreement that, "If it is to be, it is up to me," and, "If God doesn't meet my needs, then I'll have to do it for myself. In fact, it is my *right* to provide for myself if God doesn't do it." The truth is this: "If God doesn't provide it, I am infinitely better off without it." All these beliefs set me up for an avalanche of sinful behavior - which resulted in the bondage of footholds that always come from false beliefs (strongholds). If you had asked me whether or not I believed these things, I would have said "Absolutely not!", and "parroted" to you all the "right" responses I had been taught in church. This is because these beliefs were hidden in my subconscious, 'implicit' memory – hidden in blind spots. So, one stronghold led to five with no conscious effort or resistance on my part. A whole *nest* of inter-related strongholds which all supported each other were established in my mind. No wonder the Bible refers to these false beliefs as a 'stronghold'! This whole sequence of moving from one belief to the next illustrates how subtle and sneaky our own sinful natures and lack of understanding, encouraged by Satan and his helpers, can be.

Rules can be helpful in training children. But, as we mature, rules (in a spiritual context) should be used only as guidelines (necessary evils) if at all. As C. S. Lewis wrote, let's not "…mistake necessary evils for good. When we begin to consider rules as a necessary, normal part of our Christian life, we have allowed a temporary means to replace the very ends they were intended to serve."[60] Ungodly, selfish, sinful desires do need to be dealt with but *not* by rules (however well-intentioned). The mistake is easy to make. Godly desires don't need rules. The Holy Spirit empowers us 'both to will and to do' the things God wants done as we expose ourselves to Biblical truth. These need to be dealt with by replacing lies (strongholds) with truth and bondage (footholds) with freedom.

I discovered these strongholds one at a time over a period of several years. God was so gracious and strategically wise not to reveal these to me all at once. I surely would have been overwhelmed. As I recognized each stronghold, I replaced it with truth. I also recognized how godless and sinful each was and how I had been drawn into sinful behaviors by each. We not only have to intellectually see a stronghold for what it is and for the damage it has done in our life, we also have to see it for the putrid, rotten thing it is in the light of God's truth and perfection. After I had recognized the third or fourth stronghold and had seen how unexpected and rotten they really were, I began to wonder how many of these beliefs still were in blind spots waiting to be revealed. In my mind's eye, I saw myself in a boat on a lake with black water. Every so often, a rotten, putrid, bloated corpse (a stronghold) would pop to the surface of the lake. It was my job to go get it, drag it to the shore, and burn it. Yes, I'm still dragging and burning.

Each newly recognized stronghold left me feeling surprised and stunned as I saw it, for the first time, as it really was. Dan Allender calls this moment of recognition being "stunned into silence". He observes:

> What is the kind of silence that brings about a lengthy look into the eyes of God? It is the silence evoked by surprise. Few words could be more important … than surprise. There are few experiences in life that have the power to shed us of our burdensome struggles like surprise … when we're caught in our sin and painted into a corner where we cannot escape the reality of what we deserve.[61]

When we recognize the awfulness and damage done by cooperating with the enemy of our souls in believing his lies and sinning as we do, we may feel a sudden wave of self-condemnation, self loathing, or self-hatred. "How could I do that?" Recognize immediately that these thoughts and feelings are not from the Holy Spirit or from your own spirit but from the accuser of your soul, Satan, using his evil spirits. Take those thoughts captive. Renounce them, reject them. Our enemy just wants to attack you in another way. God gave you victory in one area of your life (recognizing and getting rid of a stronghold) so Satan attacks from another direction. Don't agree with his lies that you should reject, or hate, yourself, because of your past (and forgiven) sins, thoughts, or strongholds.

As I recognized several more strongholds, I began to be confronted with suggestions the enemy was making: "I'm a mess. This is going to go on forever. I'll never get free from all of these lies." Sometimes, the devil uses a combination of lies and truth to make his lies more believable. Actually, I was a 'mess'. But, I'm less of a mess now than I was then. I'm fully committed to this process of 'dragging and burning' for as long as it takes because it is all part of the way God is making me more like Jesus. It is my hope and prayer that you'll join me in this process in your own live. Someday, when I'm finally with Him, I'll never have to 'drag and burn' again. What a great day that will be!

The stronghold of, "If it is to be, it is up to me" is still a deeply rooted *habit pattern* in my life. It sets me up for a spirit of control to get a foothold in my life even though I have replaced the stronghold with truth. Far too often, I start scheming how I can get accomplished whatever it is that I'm currently focusing on. I see something that I want. So, I try to figure out how to make it happen. Here is a recent example from my life that may sound silly to you, but it illustrates what I'm talking about: I got the idea that it would be nice to put light-weight wheels and some sort of standing platform on my inflatable fly fishing pontoon boat. There is nothing wrong with having wheels and the ability to stand. The problem is that, once I start seriously focusing on something I would like to have or do, it somehow 'morphs' into a 'need'. At that point, I am tempted to allow it to become a way to make a 'happier' life for myself *now*. Too often, I don't ask God about it. I just start figuring out how to make it happen. What this points out for me (and I hope for others too) is that, once we deal with strongholds and footholds, we are still going to have to deal with our deeply ingrained thought patterns and mental habits. Someone has said that it takes a continuing effort for 28 days to break a habit. For me, it seems to take longer. Maybe I'm missing the 'continuing effort' part. There is more about dealing with habits in the chapter entitled 'Staying Free'.

The idea that, on our own, we can live a selfish, self-centered, and yet fulfilling life (however we might define that – personal happiness, money, pleasure, success, ...) is just another version of the 'do it myself' stronghold. The truth is that Jesus said we can't do that and be his disciples. We are to take up our cross and follow Him.[62] C. S. Lewis put it like this:

> The Christian way is different: harder, and easier. Christ says, "Give me all. I don't want so much of your time and so much of your money and so much of your work: I want you. I have not come to torment your natural self [sinful nature], but to kill it. No half measures are any good. I don't want to cut off a branch here and there, I want to have the whole tree down. I don't want to drill a tooth ... I want to have it out. Hand over the whole natural self, all the desires which you think are innocent as well as the ones you think wicked – the whole outfit. I will give you a new self instead. In fact, I will give you, myself: my own self shall become yours. ... The terrible thing, the almost impossible thing, is to hand over your whole self – all of your wishes and precautions – to Christ. But it is far easier than what we are all trying to do instead. For what we are trying to do is to remain we call "ourselves," to keep personal happiness as our great aim in life, and yet at the same time be "good." We are all trying to let our mind and heart go their own way – centered on money or pleasure or ambition – and hoping, in spite of this, to behave honestly and chastely and humbly. And that is exactly what Christ warned us we could not do.... He meant that we must go in for the full treatment. It is hard; but the sort of compromise we are all hankering after is harder – in fact, it is impossible. It may be hard for an egg to turn into a bird: it would be a jolly sight harder for it to learn to fly while remaining in egg. We are all like eggs at present. And

you cannot go on indefinitely being just an ordinary, decent egg. We must be hatched or go bad.... This is the whole of Christianity. There is nothing else. "[63]

Some strongholds sound 'spiritual' but are not. Here is an example of one; again, mixing truth with a lie: "I have to live a good Christian life. God helps *me* to do it." In other words, God helps us do the right things through self-effort (i.e. *we* do it and God is *our* helper). The truth is that the Holy Spirit lives in us. He provides the desire, the power and the ability to live the Christian life[64]. Jesus, through the Holy Spirit, provides the "sap" to allow us to be fruitful.[65] Our job is not to let God 'help' *us* but, rather, to simply cooperate and let Him do all He wants to do in and through us. There is something that is really important, though, about the kind of 'cooperation' we are to give Him. We can cooperate 'passively' or we can cooperate 'actively'. When we cooperate passively, we make no effort to obey what we believe God wants us to do. When we cooperate actively, we begin to obey and then God's power does it through us. In a way, it is like our Kirby vacuum cleaner. It has a power assist function that eliminates most of the effort move it back and forth. As soon as you begin to move it forward, it moves itself forward. When you stop pushing forward, it stops. A child of three could easily operate it. There is another source of power operating there 'behind the scenes'. God will do all that needs to be done in our lives. All we have to do is start moving in the direction we believe He wants us to go.

Using this same example, let's look at another way that Satan can trick us. Suppose that, this time, Satan (and/or our own sin nature) suggests that, "What really matters is that my behavior is what it should be – that it conforms to what would be Christ-like - loving God – loving people". This sounds good and I should behave in this way – it is all true! So, taken in the right way, this is a 'Godly' belief. But, if I allow it to become something *I* have to do as a duty, an obligation, or a 'law' of behavior, then, Jesus taught that it has become the 'righteousness' of the Pharisees. Once again, I've been tricked into doing the 'right' thing through self-effort to earn God's approval. He taught that what really counts are our motives and our heart attitudes[66] - i.e., being right with God through self-righteousness versus through God's righteousness. The Bible says that, "God searches our motives."[67] Everything we do has a motive behind it and every motive is based on what we think is true. As I look back on the past, there have been times when I have 'acted' lovingly toward – have helped – have served – others without truly loving them with God's kind of love in the way the Bible talks about.[68] I have taught that "we need to fake it till we make it". That is, act as if you love God or others and, sooner or later, you will begin to actually love them. Now, doing this is much better than not acting in loving ways – but, as "good" as it might be, from a human "good works" perspective, only by God living in me and through me can I truly love others. The Bible says that all our *human* works are like filthy rags in God's sight.[69] I am committed to acting in love toward others – but, I want it to be done by God's Spirit within me – not by trying to do it by my efforts alone.

Even small, relatively unimportant situations can have long-term consequences. At a Cleansing Stream retreat, a man told me, "When I was very young, we went to a family reunion. I found myself in a sea of adults I didn't know hiding behind my mother's legs. Someone noticed me doing that. My mother said, 'Oh, he is just shy'. I just remembered that happening and realized that, at that moment, I agreed with 'I am just shy'. And, I have acted painfully shy ever since then – especially among strangers. But, now, God has shown me that I am not really shy. Sometimes, I can be the life of the party." This man had been limited and damaged for most of his life by his mothers 'off-handed' comment until he recognized and removed the stronghold. Once we see the lie, then we can ask God to show us the truth.

One of my most recently discovered strongholds is: "Emotional intimacy is not safe. It is not okay to be mushy." This stronghold not only has to do with the way I show affection, but also, with trying to maintain a 'safe' emotional distance from others. I've included the journaling process of dealing with this in Appendix B. The reason I am bringing it up here is that we can often uncover the source of a stronghold by the words we choose to use when we explicitly define the lie that we have believed. I'll talk more about the 'explicit' part that below. The clue is that this stronghold was established early in my life. It is in the last word –'mushy'. This is a word a young child might use. I wouldn't normally use that word as an adult. Ask God to help you be sensitive to any clue that will help you recognize your strongholds.

There never seems to be enough time to get done everything I want done. It has taken me a lot longer to write this book, for example, than I thought it would. Late last year, while I was feeling particularly pressed by the feeling that I was somehow procrastinating and I just needed to get the book done, I 'heard' the suggestion, "I'm no spring chicken! Time is running out for me." Actually, this is, to some degree, the truth – but it is only a partial truth - which is often the most deceptive form of a lie. I was being tempted to turn this whole writing thing into a duty, an obligation, and a compulsion - something I *had* to just get done rather than allow it to be the labor of love that it is. I was being tempted to panic, to push, push, push, and to beat myself up for being so lazy. By God's grace, I was just aware enough to ask Jesus, "Lord, what is *this* about? Is this feeling from you? Is this conviction or condemnation?" As I thought about it, I realized that I was feeling guilt and condemnation. Here is a truth that you need to especially take a note of: any time you are feeling condemned, it is part of a spiritual attack – It is not from the Lord. The Bible says that, "… there is now no condemnation for those who are in Christ Jesus, because through Christ Jesus the law of the Spirit of life has set me free from the law of sin and death."[70] When God shows us something we need to deal with, He gives us a feeling of conviction (not condemnation) that leads us away from sin and back into fellowship with Him.[71] Once I recognized that this was a spiritual attack, I asked, "Lord, I am being tempted to believe a lie (establish a stronghold). What is the truth you want me to see?" I 'heard', "There is always enough time to do what *God* wants done." I replaced Satan's lie with God's truth. Whenever we replace a lie with the truth, we replace a lie (stronghold) with a Godly belief. I felt like a huge weight had been lifted off my shoulders. I was completely free from those 'specific' feelings of guilt and condemnation. I used the word 'specific' because we are subject to continuing spiritual attack. The Bible says Satan can present himself as an "angel of Light".[72] So, he'll be back under an assumed name again, sooner or later – trying to get some area of my life under his influence. Keep your spiritual armor on and use the other spiritual resources God has given you. When you do, victory is guaranteed! Isn't this amazing? This is healing! This is freedom! This is joy! This is praise! This is God's love in action! This is both knowledge and revelation!

Strongholds – part 4 - GETTING FREE FROM STRONGHOLDS
(Possible chapter title?)

I'm guessing that, given all that has been said and written above, you already have a very good Idea how get rid of strongholds and you may have already done so. Good for you! So, the primary purpose of the following is to summarize and, perhaps, reinforce what you already know. Even though a sequential process is described here, I don't want you to see this process as a 'formula'. We need to let God guide the process. We need to deal with whatever God shows us that needs correction as promptly as we can. Sometimes, I find that I will need to deal first with getting free from the bondage of a foothold as I recognize a pattern of sin in my life. Then, I will begin to look for the nest of strongholds (beliefs) that set me up to get caught in the foothold. But, sometimes, God will show me a stronghold first through reading the Bible or by reading about someone else's experience. This is not one of those "Three Steps to Happiness" or "Seven Steps to Freedom" self-help books. Discovering strongholds is a dynamic, organic process that only God can direct. Only God knows best when and how to do all that needs to be done. God wants us free from strongholds and footholds even more than we want to be free. Sometimes we ask God questions about one area of concern and God's answers lead us to another issue that He wants us to deal with first. Sometimes, God will reveal a truth to us so strongly, so absolutely, that the stronghold is torn down and replaced without the need to specifically put the lie into actual words.

Eldredge observes that the process of dealing with our brokenness [strongholds] is like dealing with an iceberg. You can chip away at what you can see and then more comes above the surface, comes into view. Then you chip away at that. Over time, and with persistence, the iceberg is gone.[73] Don't be discouraged if you discover that an area of brokenness (a tendency to sin in a particular way, a stronghold, a foothold) in your life needs to be dealt with later at a deeper level. Sometimes we deal with an area of brokenness and, "poof", it is gone forever. At other times, it seems like God wants to give us a rest and then begins to deal with the next level of our need that only He can see. Sometimes we get answers in fragments, progressively. Write down what you feel God has revealed to you. The answer (truth statements) may also come in fragments. When you get an answer, does it convey the spirit of Jesus; does it draw you to God? If not, reject it. If it does, obey it. It can take time to get clarity.[74] This can happen over a period of weeks or, even, many years. We can cooperate with this process by praying something like:

> *Lord, please continue Your work in me, to clean me up, to reveal the rotting things stuck on the bottom of the lake in my life (in my blind-spots). Lord, I want my life to be pure and holy in Your sight. Please give me patience to stick with this process.*

The things we believe guard the paths of access into our minds. It is not enough to pull down enemy strongholds. We *must* replace them with *Godly* beliefs. I am reminded of a painting by Thomas Kinkade titled *Guardian Castle*. It shows a castle guarding the path through a mountain pass. The path leads down into a beautiful, lush valley nestled in a ring of mountains. We all need 'Guardian Castles' controlling access to all the places of access into our minds.

When we become Christians, even if it is at an early age, there are many strongholds and, almost always, footholds already established. Francis Frangipane put this same idea this way:

> It is foolish to assume that our salvation experience has eliminated all the wrong ideas and attitudes – the strongholds – which are still influencing our perceptions and behavior. Yes, old things passed away, and truly new things have come, but until we are walking in the fullness of Christ, we should not assume that the process of change is over.[75]

Our strongholds and footholds follow us into our Christian life and are part of the healing that needs to happen for us to become 'whole and holy'[76]. One way to define wholeness and holiness is to be free of known sin, from strongholds, and from footholds. In writing about being whole and holy, John Eldredge observed:

> Whole and holy. The two go hand-in-hand. Oh, how important that is. You can't find the holiness you want without deep wholeness. And you can't find wholeness you want without deep holiness... The Bible says we can't hope to walk the path God would have us walk without the healing of our

souls... Healed. As in fixed. Restored. Made whole... This truth is essential to our view of the gospel. It will shape your convictions about nearly everything else. God wants to restore us. Our part is to turn, to repent as best we can. But we also need his healing. ... God chose us to make us whole and holy through his love. God will make known to us the path of life [that leads to] wholeness and holiness.[77]

Cleansing Stream ministries puts it this way:

A lot of these beliefs about yourself, the world, and others come from the things you were told as a child. Children accept the words spoken to them much more eagerly than adults. Those early seeds can form vast root systems that either help you or hurt you as you grow up. The good news is you can uproot Satan's seed – pull up the whole plant by the roots – and remove it completely by the power of the Holy Spirit... A seed that has been received and retained will automatically reproduce. The words that you have accepted and nurtured will likewise bring a harvest. This can be good news or bad news depending upon the seed. As a Christian, though, it is important to remember God's grace and mercy are available to cover all of your mistakes and heal all of your wounds. Nothing is too difficult for him... His power is greater than anything... You do not have to receive words that go against what the Bible has declared to be true about you. The word of God and words that are consistent with it are the only seeds that need to remain in your life. You can refuse bad seeds and plant good ones in their place, seeds that will reproduce a harvest of righteousness and confidence in the Lord. Sow and grow orchards of love, joy, peace, and patience![78]

When we discover strongholds and replace them with truth, we are pulling up plants that come from bad seed and replacing them with good seed that will *eventually* produce the fruit of righteousness. I used the word 'eventually' because, as you already know, it takes time for a seed to germinate, grow a plant, and produce fruit. Our enemy wants us to get impatient and start trying to produce 'fruit' on our own without God's help or timing. That kind of fruit is poison – pride, envy, self-righteousness, impatience … Whenever we are working with God to get free, Satan will try to maintain his control on us by joining in with the healing process to push us to get healed in a way or in a time that is not what God wants done. For me, it usually has to do with God's timing. I want what I want '*now*'. This is the time-focus of my God-given temperament. It is a strength – when I don't overuse it. The problem is, too often I do. Whenever I recognize this 'now' thing trying to take over again, I usually pray something like this:

> *Lord, I acknowledge the sin of impatience. Please forgive me and heal me of 'now' so I will be willing to take the time to ask you and wait for your answer and your timing. Lord, help me to be satisfied with steady progress – net gain – and not be compulsively driven for results 'now'.*

This brings up another caution. We must not allow ourselves to get tricked into trying to deal with characteristics in our lives that are actually miss-used or over-used parts of your God-given temperament. These traits are not usually strongholds. Rather, simply, confess whatever it is – if it is sinful. We must not try to get rid of God-given strengths in ourselves simply because we have a tendency to over-use or miss-use them. Eldredge says it this way:

> You can't repent your way out of brokenness. It simply doesn't work. We repent of our sins; the brokenness must be healed.[79]

This kind of healing is discussed in more detail later in this chapter. As we receive and apply more and more truth in our lives and healing happens, we learn to use our strengths more appropriately, and get rid of the lies we have been agreeing with, we are becoming more and more like the person God created us to be – Himself![80]

Jesus said, "When a strongman, fully armed, guards his own house, his possessions are safe. But when someone stronger attacks and overpowers him, he takes away the armor in which the man trusted and divides up the spoils."[81] The 'strong man' Jesus was talking about in this parable was Satan. Spiritual warfare is all about taking away Satan's armor. What exactly is this armor that protects Satan? The armor on which demons rely is our own *thoughts, attitudes, and opinions* which are in agreement with evil.[82] In other words, Satan's various pieces of armor are the strongholds we have believed! When we replace strongholds with truth, Satan's armor is taken away – piece by piece!

We have quoted extensively from Dr. Lehman's book, *Outsmarting Yourself*, in chapter two to help us understand how and why we fall prey to strongholds and footholds so easily. Dr. Lehman also writes about a way of relating to others that he calls 'attunement':

> *Attunement is an especially important form of interpersonal emotional connection. I am successfully offering attunement if I see you correctly, understand your internal experience, join you in the emotions you're experiencing, genuinely care about you, and am glad to be with you; and you have successfully received my attunement if you feel seen, heard, and understood, if you feel that I am with you in your experience, and if you feel that I care about you and that I am glad to be with you.*[83]

Most of us probably think about this way of relating to others as *empathy*. Counselors and therapists try to 'attune' to their clients. But, notice that attunement involves both *offering* and *receiving*. The only one who can truly and completely attune to us is God; but, with His help, we can, at least, try to attune to others *and to ourselves* in this way. When we feel we are in an environment where someone else is attuned to us and we accept their attunement, we feel more relaxed and safe than when we feel we are in a hostile environment. When we feel 'attuned' to by God or others and receive that attunement, we are much better able to hear what God wants us to hear.

As we seek to recognize strongholds and replace them with truth, we will be able to do it much more easily when we recognize and receive the truth that God is fully attuned to us. He loves us with a perfect love and guides us in this process. As we go through this process, we also need to offer attunement to, and receive attunement from, *ourselves*. This is not easy to do – especially when our strongholds and footholds involve beliefs about ourselves that result in a limited ability or unwillingness to see ourselves from God's perspective. He has the ability to see us *through* our relationship with Jesus; to see us as His perfect children living eternally with Him. In this context, we can offer to and receive attunement from ourselves. We can then deal with our self-condemnation, self-hatred, and self-rejection by recognizing and confessing these sins. Knowing that we are completely forgiven and safely in God's care, we can enter into this process without fear or worry about anything but getting free from our strongholds, our footholds, and having our hurtful memories healed, which we will discuss in the next chapter.

So now, let's summarize this process in a step by step way – remembering that this is not a 'formula' – but, rather, a list of things to be sure we have covered as we work our way through the process. Don't forget that we use spiritual weapons to demolish strongholds.[84] These weapons are the resources we discussed in chapter three. They are available to us only because God makes them available. It is only because God has revealed something to us that has helped us recognize a need for freedom in a specific area of our life. Sometimes, God gives us just a fragment of an idea that needs clarified and, sometimes, He gives us a blinding flash of insight. Either way, try to cover all the steps in the process. But, don't worry, God will be sure to show you if you've missed something important for your specific need.

1. Pray first. This whole process needs to be bathed in prayer. Ask for protection from enemy interference. Satan will sidetrack us if he can – if we let him. He doesn't want us free. The fewer strongholds and footholds we have, the more dangerous we are to his plans for us and others; and, the more effective warriors we become in fighting the battles we are all faced with. Pray for God's guidance and wisdom to focus on what He wants to deal with in His priorities and timing. Ask God questions to reveal what He wants you to recognize and do next. Keep asking for clarification and direction as this process continues. These prayers don't have to be fancy or long. Keep them conversational. But, make them as specific as possible. God already knows the worst about us and loves us anyway. Our attitudes and motives are what really matter. Then, follow through and obey any revelation you receive from God.

2. Confess and repent of any known sin. 1 John 1:9 says, that, as we confess our sin, God will forgive that sin and cleanse from *all* unrighteousness. Don't root around for sin to confess in your life – God will reveal to you anything you need to confess. Confession and repentance is part of getting free from both strongholds and footholds. Known sin must be acknowledged and confessed before

there can be forgiveness and real transformation.[85] We need to be sure that we are not harboring any known unforgiveness towards God, others, or ourselves. For some of us, it is hard to believe that God really forgives us. I found a good example of this in a quote from the Discovery Series, *The Forgiveness of God*, from RBC ministries. A person was struggling about whether or not God could really forgive her. She continued to struggle with not *feeling* forgiven by God. She said,

> "I pled with the Father to help me. The Bible had become a staff of life to me so I turned to it in desperation. Was it true? Was I truly forgiven for all my sins? God led me to these verses: 'Do not remember the former things, nor consider the things of old. Behold, I will do a new thing, now it shall spring forth; shall you not know it? I will even make a road in the wilderness and rivers in the desert. I, even I, am he who blots out your transgressions for my own sake; and I will not remember your sentence (Isaiah 43:18–19, 25)'. My heart welled up with joy. My smile returned, for I knew I was forgiven and that I didn't have to remember who I used to be. I realize that I am the Lords – for his glory and praise".[86]

> Notice that, in the process of confession and repentance, God led this lady to recognize both a stronghold and the truth statement without her even being conscious of the process she had just gone through.

3. Unforgiveness towards others also includes forgiving our ancestors for all the sinful influences they passed on to us. Usually, we don't even know what most of these influences are. We need to forgive our ancestors for *any* generational influences (known or unknown). We must not try to use any of these influences as excuses for our own sinfulness. These 'generational influences' include any vows or agreements our ancestors may have made that bind or commit their future generations in some way to sinful or demonic influence or control. These kinds of vows and agreements are often associated with fraternal organizations (such as some college or other fraternities, Masonic organizations, or even actual satanic worship). Unforgiveness binds us to those we refuse to forgive. Forgiveness frees us from these

connections and influences. You might want to pray something like this:

> *In Jesus name, I forgive the generations that have come before me for all sinful influences they have passed on to me, known or unknown; and, I break any ungodly vows, agreements, or commitments made by those who are related to me generationally that have bound me in any way to sinful or demonic influence or control. I also break any ungodly vows, agreements, or commitments made by my ancestors or myself with all others to whom they or I have been under any spiritual authority.*

4. Repent for, renounce, and break all known footholds. This process is described in the last chapter. The reason this is done at this time is to stop any known, established, demonic attachments, influence, or control in our lives as a result of our own sinful behaviors. Getting rid of our known footholds also helps us recognize and deal with the strongholds and memories that need to be healed more easily.

5. Get rid of (confess and repent for) any specific demonic influences that you know about – including past involvements with things or practices associated with demonic activity. This includes things like: Ouija boards, séances, palm reading, various forms of fortune-telling (like use of a crystal ball or reading of tea leaves), satanic worship, study of or participation in witchcraft related activities, shamanism… Again, don't go rooting around. Allow God to show you anything he wants you to deal with.

6. Ask God to show you the specific thoughts and actual words of the lie or, more often, lies you have believed. As you identify or recognize the lie, write it down in your journal so you won't miss any part of your revelation. Occasionally, recognizing the actual words of the lie seems unnecessary when you have clearly seen and embraced the truth. Let God guide you in this.

7. Write down a 'truth-statement' to replace the lie(s). This statement must be based on Biblical truth as completely and accurately as possible. Very often, we will discover the truth, at least in an embryonic form, before we recognize the lie it is intended to replace. As we read the Bible, or are exposed to other sources of truth, some thought or truth (*rhema*) will 'jump out' at us. Note the sources of the insight.

It may be a valuable reference if you need to follow up later. Try to make sure the truth statement completely addresses each element of the stronghold. If a stronghold has not been identified in detail, ask God to show it to you. This kind of prayer is simply a conversation with God. It is a free-flowing back and forth activity. We can keep asking God as many questions as needed until we have clarity. We don't need to be in any hurry. Once you think you really have the truth statement in detail, live with it a while. Read it carefully. Pray about it. Lay it down and come back to it later. Edit it as needed. Visualize what it will be like, what it will mean in your life when the lie is fully replaced with this truth. How will it feel? This process may take some time. Enjoy the process. When I first became aware of strongholds and footholds, *rhema* statements of truth from God weren't even on my radar as a resource. But, talking to and hearing from God is the key to dealing with strongholds and footholds most successfully – thank the Lord for His *rhema* guidance.

8. Intentionally replace the lie with the truth. Once you have a written statement of both the lie(s) and the truth, intentionally, specifically, with your will engaged, in Jesus' name, replace the lie with the truth. Pray something like this:

> *Lord, thank you for showing me both the lies I have believed and the truth You want them replaced with. Now, in Jesus name, I replace the lie that (fill in the blank) with the truth that (fill in the blank).*

It is really that simple. With God's authority, power, and our position in Jesus (along with our other spiritual resources), Satan's strongholds really are torn down.[87]

We can be absolutely sure that this is true at both a spiritual and an intellectual level. But, at a 'feeling' level, it sometimes seems less true. If that is true for you, to the degree that you are able, try to visualize a stronghold constructed from the lie(s) being replaced. Then, visualize a big grappling hook or a wrecking ball made from the truth statement totally reducing the lie(s) to complete rubble. Then, stomp the rubble into dust under your feet. Finally, re-build a beautiful castle constructed from the truth statement over the place where the stronghold used to be. Doing this kind of visualization exercise might feel strange the first few times you do it. But, for me, somehow it makes the total destruction of the stronghold made of lies, and its replacement with truth, seem even more real.

9. Take thoughts captive. Once the truth is firmly established in our thinking, we will begin to recognize the temptations from our sin nature, other's sin natures, and Satan that we didn't recognize before. Instead of going ahead and sinning (and further strengthening the bondage of footholds) we will begin to reject those thoughts. The Bible calls this 'taking thoughts captive and making them obedient to Christ'. Let me give you a mental picture of this process that I hope will stick with you: A sinful thought or temptation surfaces in your consciousness. You recognize it for what it really is. It is the same as if someone threw a hand grenade into your foxhole. You pick it up quickly and throw it right back before it explodes. The only difference is that this is a 'thought'-grenade. When this kind of thought enters my mind, I say something like this out loud and with my eyes open – I'm not praying - I'm kicking demon butt in Jesus' name:

Satan (spirit of lust, or whatever it is that is tempting me), get out of my mind! In Jesus' name, I reject your thought.

Sometimes, Satan then runs around to the other ear with condemnation, "What kind of Christian do you think you are? Thinking thoughts like that. Shame on you!" When he does that, I just tell him,

"Buzz off, Satan! What I just experienced was 'victory' – not something to be condemned for."

Don't forget, our thoughts need to be spoken out loud when we are breaking the control of a stronghold, or foothold, or taking thoughts captive because our enemy Satan and his helpers can't read the unspoken thoughts of a Christian because God the Holy Spirit lives in us.[88] A demonic spirit cannot live in a Christian or know his or her thoughts because God already lives there. Break habits of thought. We'll discuss this in more detail in the *Staying Free* chapter. Once we have gotten rid of demonic influence in a specific area of our lives, we usually then will have to deal with our habitual thought patterns. God will provide both the will and the ability to do this effectively as we cooperate with Him. One of our best reminders to keep working on our habitual thought patterns is when we have to keep on taking the same thought captive. Eventually, this will happen less often. But, in my experience, Satan never fully gives up even when we never let him win.

10. Finally, memories that contain damaging or toxic content need to be healed. Allow God to heal these hurtful, toxic memories that are still 'festering' like some hidden infected wound in our past. Healing of these memories is discussed next.

MEMORIES

"Now the Lord is the Spirit, and where the Spirit of the Lord is, there is freedom. And we all, who with unveiled faces contemplate the Lord's glory, are being transformed into his image with ever increasing glory, which comes from the Lord, who is the Spirit."[1]

The Apostle Paul

Throughout our lives, we all accumulate unresolved traumatic memories. Some, we simply don't remember consciously. Some, we remember but they seem inconsequential. Some are so terrible that we wish we couldn't remember them at all. As we approach the process of having our memories healed, we need to let God decide which ones we need to deal with first. Whatever memory comes into our awareness may be what God wants to heal next. Nothing is too small, silly, or embarrassing if the Holy Spirit brings it into your awareness.[2] Remember that a toxic memory can include anything that has happened to us or perhaps not happened to us that should have. The real issue is not that bad things have happened or good things have not, but rather that we have misunderstood what happened at the time and believed untrue explanations for them. We tend to focus on the *pain* we felt at the time and often don't recognize the lies (strongholds) we believed to explain why these things happened to us. The obvious, big issues may not yield to healing until smaller issues are resolved or visa versa; only Jesus knows which ones these are and when and how to deal with each. Healing of toxic memories happens when we see and accept what really happened from God's perspective.

The Bible tells us that God can use everything that happens to us for our good.[3] This includes the things that were obviously bad at the time. One example of this truth is the Bible story of Joseph.[4] Joseph's brothers were jealous of him and sold him into slavery in Egypt. Through a series of amazing circumstances and 'coincidences', Joseph became the ruler of

Egypt, second only to the Pharaoh. Because of a great famine throughout the middle-east, Joseph's brothers came to Egypt to buy food and were brought to Joseph but they didn't recognize him. Joseph didn't tell them who he was at first. After his brothers had made several trips to and from Egypt to buy food, Joseph finally revealed to his brothers who he was. Of course, they were terrified. The story ends with Joseph telling his brothers, "Don't be afraid. Am I in the place of God? You intended to harm me, but God intended it for good to accomplish what is now being done, the saving of many lives."[5] Joseph understood the truth that God can and will use even the most terrible things that happen in our lives for our highest good if we will let Him.

This might be a good place to talk about 'time travel'. When we remember an experience of a situation in our past that we're still feeling the hurt, pain, anger, resentment, jealousy, fear, ... from a memory, we can ask Jesus to go back to that experience with us and help us understand what was going on from His perspective. We can ask Him what He wants us to know about it. These kinds of damaging memories almost always involve (or once involved) strongholds and footholds in our lives. Jesus has the ability to 'travel back in time' with us in our memories and help us recognize that He was there with us in that situation. He can help us see the lies we believed (the agreements we made) at that time. He can show us the truth that we need to see now to get rid of those lies. He can help us see the spiritual bondage that was established because we believed those lies. These kinds of experiences happen to us simply because we live in a sin-sick, cursed world, at war spiritually, and influenced by Satan. God may even help us see the real purposes of those experiences. As God helps us process those experiences, the damaging feelings and beliefs associated with them will no longer be able to get us so stirred up when something happens to us that brings up those feelings or that resurfaces those memories. When Jesus enters the memory, the way we see and remember the memory changes. He reveals new truth and a new perspective. As a result, our feelings about the memory also changes. It becomes less toxic with Jesus present. Eldredge expresses it this way:

> Inner healing might be described as sanctifying the past, inviting Jesus back into events and relationships, because for one reason or another he was not invited in at the time. I love that thought - sanctifying the past. Now that we are walking

with Jesus, we can invite him into our past and walk with him there too. Much of our hearts were shaped "back then", most of our deep convictions formed.[6]

There is another thing that is worth knowing as we remember hurtful experiences in our lives: Even though we may not have been aware of it at the time, God was there with us experiencing all the pain and hurt we were experiencing at that time. That is a very comforting truth for me and, I hope, for you too. God has personally suffered betrayal, torture, hurt, jealousy... and so much more. God the Father and God the Holy Spirit felt everything Jesus felt as He was being crucified. They felt the joy He felt as He rose from the dead – knowing all that He had accomplished for us by what He had just done. God feels the pain we feel because He lives in us through the Holy Spirit just as He did in Jesus. Our suffering is his suffering too. Because we are Christians, we have fellowship with him. We are becoming more and more like him.[7] As we do this, we have the 'mind of Christ' developing in us to a greater and greater degree.[8] This means that we will also begin to feel what He feels – be hurt by what hurts Him – made joyful by what He enjoys. This is a form of empathy, unity, oneness, and intermixing of lives with God that that I want to become more and more a reality in my life. It's my hope and prayer that you want this too. This is a privilege that is deeper and more profound than most of us can realize. It is like being drawn to touch a million volt high-power line that we would only dare to touch it if we knew that we wouldn't be hurt by it. An airplane that is hit by lightning is rarely damaged in any way because it is "above ground". We can safely "touch" the heart of God because we are not "grounded" – not part of this world. Thank you Lord!!

We learned from Dr. Lehman's insights in chapter two that, when hurtful things happen to us, memories can be established in our implicit (invisible) memories that contain toxic content – thoughts, ideas, and beliefs that can damage our relationships with others, with God, and with how we see ourselves. There is a natural fear associated with revisiting old memories[9]; the very experiences that were so painful and resulted so often in strongholds and bondage - the pain of confusion, fear of rejection, fear of abuse, fear of not being in control, fear of not measuring up, fear of being without help, feelings of shame, of panic, of self hatred… None of us wants to go back into memories like these and re-experience the pain.

The difference this time is that we are going back with an all-powerful and all-wise God who loves us more than we can imagine and who has chosen which experience we're going back to for the purpose of healing. We are also going there with Jesus to dig out any leftover lies we believed at that time and replace them with truth if they haven't already been dealt with. In Dr. Lehman's language, we are going back to 'reprocess' those memories in the light of God's presence and truth. He explains:

> When we are able to successfully complete this processing journey, we get through the painful experience without being traumatized – we emotionally and cognitively "metabolize" the experience in a healthy way, and instead of having any toxic power in our lives, the adequately processed painful experience contributes to our knowledge, skills, empathy, wisdom, and maturity. That is, when we successfully process a painful experience, we don't just stuff it down into our subconscious, or teach ourselves to think about other things. We actually get through it stronger and wiser.[10]

We need God to lead us in the process of going back into those memories so He can heal the toxic content they contain. It is important to ask both God and ourselves honest, unedited questions. God wants us to understand. He can handle our anger, our confusion, our doubt … God wants us not only to share our hearts with Him but, also, to be honest with ourselves. Ask God questions. Just talk to Him. "Lord, which memory do you want to work with this time? Jesus, please come into this memory with me. Father God, help me see whatever You want me to see. Please heal whatever needs healing. God, where were You when this happened? Lord, how could you have allowed such terrible things to happen? Jesus, where were you in this memory? Lord, what do you want to say to me about this experience?" Ask yourself questions, "What memories do I have of painful, hurtful, embarrassing… situations or experiences? What conclusion or message did I believe or accept as a result of those experiences? What vows did I make? What is the truth, given what I now know?" Allow yourself to remember the experience as vividly and with as much detail as possible. Through this process, we can get at least partial answers to the questions we all tend to ask about these experiences. It is especially helpful if you have someone available who is experienced with successfully helping others experience this process (a

Christian friend, prayer partner, life coach, mentor, counselor, pastor, or therapist), to work with you and coach you. Be sure to journal the insights and understandings you receive so you don't forget them. Ask more questions as they occur to you. Follow along with the theme of what God is revealing to you. Later, you can review your journal, reaffirm, and, perhaps, refine your understandings. John Eldredge describes the experience of having our memories healed in this way:

> As you are inviting Jesus into your wounds, what is so very beautiful is the fact that quite often – not every time, but more than you'll expect – Jesus will show you what he is doing; you will see him come. Call it seeing with your mind's eye or Christ using your imagination or seeing with the eyes of your heart or your spirit – however you want to describe it. Often you will see Christ come back into your past. He may take you by the hand and lead you out of that room. You might see him step between you and the one who wounded you, or he might simply tell you, *you are forgiven, you are safe, I love you.* Healing doesn't necessarily have to be dramatic. Oftentimes it is very quiet. Jesus simply comes as we invite him to, and though we may not "see" him or "hear" him, he comes, and we sense a new peace or quietness in our soul. Our heart feels better somehow. The important thing for us is to give him permission to enter these wounded places, invite his healing love, and wait in prayer for him to come. Do this with each memory of wounding, with each event (ask the Holy Spirit to guide). Often I will pray Isaiah 61... Many times Jesus simply says, "I love you." We need to open our hearts up to his love. As we do, it allows him to come to this very place. Linger there and listen; asked for the healing grace of Jesus Christ over and over again. He comes, dear friends, he comes.[11]

Over-reactions and unexpected emotions are gifts from God to help us discover something that needs to be healed. When you know you have over-reacted to some situation, first, confess your sin (if sin was involved), then, invite Jesus into the moment to help you understand why – even as you also apologize to whoever you may have unloaded on. Healing the past involves both repentance and healing.[12] When unexpected emotions surface, do the same. If you have already revisited a related memory with

Jesus and have received healing, He may be showing you that you need some additional, deeper healing. So, ask Him more questions. Wait for the answers. Add the questions and answers to your journal. Eldredge observes:

> … Issues in me that need inner healing just sort present themselves. I don't usually go looking for them. They sort of find me. Usually through unwelcome emotions... or some old memory shows up... and that is the moment where we choose to walk with God. Don't blow past it – invite Christ in. Listen. Follow the trail.[13]

When I first read the above quote, I was reminded of several events in my past and how important acceptance and significance in others eyes had been for me. I recognized that these memories and my priorities were something I needed to pray about. I recorded my prayer in a journal. It is an example of the kinds of prayers we might choose to pray when we recognize a need.

> *Lord, I repent for seeking love and acceptance in the wrong places and for the wrong reasons. I have also been wrong for equating acceptance with significance. Lord, clarify within me exactly what significance is in Your eyes. I know I am significant to You. Help me put significance in the eyes of others in its proper place. It has been far too important to me in the past. I repent for that. Please enter into the past with me and heal both these memories and the shame related to them (when I felt that I didn't "measure up"). Lord please heal things related to this that I still don't understand.*

At the time I prayed this prayer, I didn't understand the importance of also listening for and journaling what Jesus wanted me to 'see' about the memories. But, I feel He provided the healing I needed at that time anyway by guiding what I prayed. God honors our heart-felt attempts to reach out to Him – whether we have our theology, our language, or our approach to Him 'just right' or not. He simply says, "Seek me and you will find Me."[14] When we seek and find Him, healing happens. Our heart attitude is what counts. Again, I want to stress that this whole process of getting free and getting healed needs to be a dynamic, organic process guided by God. We might remember a memory we want to ask God to help us with as a result of getting rid of a stronghold or a foothold. Or, we might discover a stronghold as part of asking God questions about an experience. Remember, no 'formulas'. Regardless of which kind of freedom or healing comes first, the most important thing is that we truly 'hear' the *truth*; that we agree with that truth; that we establish it in our minds, in our awareness, in our inner-most being. The *truth* is what will ultimately set us free by whatever process God chooses.[15]

Our unexpected reactions can also come from long-established sinful mental habits that simply (but, sometimes, not easily) need to be broken. Breaking habits is our responsibility – using the resources God has provided, of course. But, doing so requires focused, concentrated, long-term effort on our part. A sinful habit that needs to be broken is a set of behaviors or way of thinking that has been established by our *own* repeated, long-term, *personal* cooperation with our own sin nature and, usually, satanic influence. This is true whether we consciously recognized it or not as it was happening. A sinful habit, just like a good habit, is part of *us* (our deeply integrated biological brain and spiritual soul). It is not a separate spiritual entity or influence that we can simply tell to leave, or a lie (stronghold) we can replace with truth, or a bondage to demonic influence (foothold) we can simply break using God's authority and power. It is a part of *us* that we need to deal with. The breaking of sinful habits is an important subject that will be discussed in more detail in the next chapter – Staying Free.

Dr. Lehman, and nearly all of those who help others go through this process, has observed that a few key things are essential to success in having our memories healed. One of these elements includes having a real, vital, personal connection with Jesus as we re-visit a memory with Him. Dr. Lehman refers to this kind of a relationship as a 'contingent' (give and take) communication. The ideas related to this kind of relationship were discussed in chapter three. Briefly, a contingent communication with Jesus is one in which we *sense* that we are experiencing a real-time, interactive connection with Him in the present - having Him respond to us in a way that is directly related to (contingent upon) what we are mutually experiencing and communicating. This kind of connection with another person also involves the idea of 'attunement' we discussed in an earlier chapter – the *feeling* that we have mutually seen, heard, and understood each other, that we care about each other, and that we are glad to be together. There was a time in my own walk with God when I thought that having this kind of a relationship with God was reserved for a few 'spiritual giants', if it was even possible at all. But I have since come to understand that this is a relationship that is available to us all as we enter into God's process of using the resources He has given us, listening for and responding to His *rhema* communications with us, breaking the bondage to satanic influence, replacing the lies we become aware of with truth, and having our traumatic memories healed. This is the long-term process you are almost certainly involved in now because you are still reading this book. When we re-enter a memory with Jesus in this way, the healing of the toxic content in our memories is just a matter of time and sticking with God's process.

It would be wonderful if we all could experience this kind of connection with God every moment of every day. But this has not been my personal experience or that of anyone one else I know of. It seems to take a concentrated focus – intentionally turning our heart and attention toward God. Like all things we can learn to do, the more we work on, practice, and experience this, the easier it becomes. Dr. Lehman suggests that, as we are inviting Jesus into a memory, it is helpful for us to also recall a memory from a previous 'contingent' and 'attuned' connection with the Lord.[16] If you are thinking, "I don't know if I have ever had this kind of connection with God", be assured, you have – you just didn't realize it at the time. Ask God to show you when these times have happened. You will be truly encouraged and blessed as you recognize these times – both in the past and in the present. Don't look for a time when lights were flashing and bells were ringing (spiritually speaking), although, that might have been your experience. Most often, these times happen as we are quietly seeking God – during private worship or devotional times, reading the Bible, talking with a friend, mentor, or counselor, reading a book, while journaling… Sometimes, the difference between recognizing these connections with God and not recognizing them is simply knowing that they can and do happen. Just ask God to show you when they have happened in your life. When He does, that 'showing', in *itself,* will be one of those contingent and attuned experiences!

After we have gone back into memories with Jesus and have experienced healing, we can see that these 'wounding events' (memories) can become tools in God's hand to bring healing and greater compassion and understanding not only in our own lives but, also, in the lives of others too. We need to also recognize that there may be losses that we need to grieve at this point. Unfortunately, the healing of our memories doesn't change what actually happened in the past. Perhaps we made decisions that have had painful consequences. Some of these events were not our fault or the result of our decisions – but the losses are still very real. When we believed lies in the midst of our pain, we didn't experience the good that would have come if we had only been able to process the events in a healthy way. God will guide us through this part of our healing process too if we will just ask and allow Him to. We need to allow ourselves to grieve the losses in our past even as we recognize that God waited to heal the affects of those events until we were ready, had the capacity, and, perhaps, had help from a counselor or a mentor. This too is a gift of God's grace.

This brief discussion about the healing of our memories is intended to let you know that this is a part of the healing process that is available to all of us and to encourage you to experience it for ourselves if we haven't already done so. There are many excellent books that discuss the healing of memories. Dr. Lehman's book, *Outsmarting Yourself* is one of them. This book can be particularly helpful for those who feel called to or who are currently active in helping others work through this part of the healing process. Reference to other books about healing memories are also included in Appendix A

Sometimes all that is left to heal in a memory after you have recognized the lies and dealt with the footholds related to the memory is the healing of the leftover pain of betrayal, rejection, failure... The final step in healing memories is to ask the Lord to heal the broken, bruised places in our hearts. Eldredge correctly observes that the healing of our broken hearts will often include grieving the things we've lost at the time, or since, the painful experience happened. Sometimes, that original heartbreak was only the first of many related heartbreaks. Tears may flow. It is only right that they might. Deep and profound healing is often accompanied by matching emotions. Eldredge writes:

> ...let your grief happen. Use your journal to record it.
> ...Ask the Lord to heal your broken heart. Invite him into
> that place in your heart, to cleanse, to heal, and to mend. Pray

through Isaiah 61:1-3. Ask him to do those very things for you, for this place in your heart. He will. It's what he said he came to do: "Blessed are those who mourn, for they *will* be comforted." (Matt. 5:4, emphasis added).[17]

Don't forget that, if you feel stuck or blocked or lose your sense that Jesus is with you and guiding you in the healing of an especially painful memory, stop and immediately recall the memory of a time when you felt and deeply appreciated Jesus' presence with you. Spend time enjoying this memory. You can always come back to the memory healing process at another time. Jesus is the only one who can guide us through the process of healing our toxic memories. Never try it on your own without a sense of His actual, personal presence with you guiding the process. Always end every time of dealing with footholds, strongholds, or toxic memories by returning to a strong sense of Jesus' presence with you. His presence *is* always with you. Take the time often to acknowledge and appreciate it.

Ask God if there is anything else related to the memory that you are working on with Him that he wants you know about or follow-up on. Have you truly forgiven yourself and others? Have all the strongholds and footholds been addressed? Have the understandings and insights you have received been journaled? Sometimes, you may have a sense that there is more to be accomplished later – perhaps a deeper healing or other insights to be seen. Make a note of this too. God will complete all the healing that is needed in His own time and way. We just need to stay open to the process.

Staying Free

Our walk with God involves two steps: faith and obedience. We can follow God for the rest of our lives by repeating those two steps.[1]

God desires truth in our innermost parts.[2] Then you will know the truth, and the truth will set you free.[3]

Now the Lord is the Spirit, and where the Spirit of the Lord is there is freedom. And we, who with unveiled faces all reflect the Lord's glory, are being transformed into His likeness with ever increasing glory...[4]

I've got some bad news for you that you probably already know and some good news that you may not know. The bad news? Bad stuff happens in everyone's life —sometimes really bad stuff. The good news? In a Christian's life, God uses everything for our highest good[5] – even the really bad stuff. Once we see life for what it really is, understand the truth, and begin to act on that truth, then, the *real* battle begins. The enemy will do all that he can to discourage and oppose our decision to follow truth. He will try variations on the original lies (strongholds) to try to get us back under his control. He'll cause as many problems in our lives as he is allowed to. Remember the story about Job? Well, maybe not to that extreme. Job was a special case – but, you get the idea. Problems will happen. Don't be surprised![6] Jesus said, "In this world you will have trouble.[7]

The apostle Paul was another extreme case. He was an early Christian missionary and church planter. He was used by God to write almost half of the books In the New Testament. The problems most of us experience don't even begin to compare to what the apostle Paul experienced; health problems, beatings, arrests, persecution, imprisonment, ship wreck...

and, in the end, he was martyred. But, Paul said it was going to be worth it all. He wrote, "... we are heirs – heirs of God and co-heirs with Christ, if indeed we share in his sufferings in order that we may also share in his glory. I consider that our present sufferings are not worth comparing with the glory that will be revealed in us."[8] We are not like glow-sticks – they produce a faint glow, but, only when they are broken. Our problems don't have to break us but they can allow us to shine with more and more glory. God's ultimate purpose for us is that we become "pure, blameless children of God without fault, shining like stars."[9] That's a lot more light than a glow-stick!

This all sounds pretty depressing and discouraging. We can expect trouble now and 'pie in the sky by and by'. Someone has said that 'Life is hard and then you die.' Yes, life can be hard and bad stuff does happen. And, when it does, it hurts. For most of us, the hurts and bad stuff are a very small part of our total life experience. Some people focus primarily on the bad stuff and, for them, life *is* depressing and discouraging. But, for those of us who walk with God, the bad things that happen are mere bumps along the path of life that leads into an unimaginably wonderful eternity with God and each other.

We are biologically designed in a way that allows us to react quickly and, sometimes, take super-human action for a short time in the face of danger. We call this our 'fight or flight' response. This ability is a gift and a blessing from God. But, if we live our lives in a way that encourages this response on a long-term basis (i.e., always fearful that bad stuff is going to happen any second), then what can be a blessing becomes destructive. Strongholds, footholds and toxic memories create stress and fear in our minds and bodies which can result in a constant flow of chemicals in our bodies that, although may be helpful in the short-term, are toxic in the long-term. Sooner or later, long-term stress will destroy our spiritual, mental, emotional, and physical health. When we get rid of the things in our lives that separate us from God, we will then better able to trust Him. We won't be constantly stirred up by a long-term fight or flight response. We'll be healthier in every way.

If we are going to deal with the problems in our lives in healthy ways, it is very important that we recognize that the things that go wrong in our lives *are* really there to help us grow. The Bible tells us to consider it pure joy when we face trials of many kinds because the trials result in perseverance, growth, and Christian maturity.[10] In other words, there is actually purpose and meaning in the things that happen to us. "Meaning is not a luxury for us. It is a sort of spiritual oxygen which enables our souls to live."[11] The struggles in our lives may eventually make sense – with 20/20 hindsight. But, usually, we don't see why things are happening the way they do while they are happening. I'm finally starting to be more comfortable with living in a story that I don't always understand. Sure, I know the big narrative line and how it will all come out in the end. But, I don't always see how the individual events in my life fit into the big story. That's okay. It is just part of the 'adventure'. When out troubles are seen from this perspective, potentially damaging stress transforms into motivation for achievement, fulfillment, growth, joy…

The things that go wrong in our lives really do have a purpose – they are not just random events. The way we respond to these problems reveals patterns in our thinking, something important about our heart, something God is after. John Eldredge refers to our little problems as 'nits' and our big problems as 'dragons'[12]. Job experienced a whole 'herd' of dragons.

When things go wrong - when problems happen (especially the dragons), the first thing most of us do is ask God to take the problems away. And, if He doesn't do it immediately, then, we usually begin to ask God the wrong questions, "God, how could you let this happen to me? Is this my reward for trying to act on Your truth? What do You want *me* to do?" We immediately try to figure out how *we* (through our own efforts) can solve the problem. We are now at a very important fork in the road. We will either try to escape or solve our problems by doing it ourselves or we will trust God to show us what he is up to. At this point, we need ask God a different kind of question with a different attitude, "What is going on here Lord? What do you want me to see? Have I strayed back into my old ways without realizing it? Is there something in my life or my thinking that You want to deal with? Is there a deeper healing that You want to do?" John Eldredge describes his personal experience this way:

> …sometimes God wants to speak to me about something entirely different from the question I am asking. If I don't get an answer on the subject I've raised, I may need to ask a different

question. You'll find this very helpful in learning to walk with God. If He doesn't seem to be answering the question you are asking, stop, and ask Him what he does want to speak to. It's not what God is *not* giving, but what he *is* giving... [that we need to look for].[13]

We can sometimes unconsciously full back into things we thought we had dealt with 'once–and–four–all'. Does that mean that this process of breaking strongholds and footholds only works temporarily? No. It means that we still have a sin nature that trips us up more often than we realize. When this happens, we might need to re-visit old issues and deal with them again if needed. It can also mean that we have grown in our understanding of the issues we have dealt with and now need to deal with them again at a deeper level. Either way, don't be fooled by the enemy's lies that, "This spiritual warfare stuff doesn't work – I might as well just forget about it and get on with getting all I can out of this life in any way I can". Just take *this* thought captive and throw it right back into Satan's face. Revisit whatever needs to be dealt with again and continue your growth in the freedom process.

Given that God is working in our lives through all that happens to us and that we rarely understand God's purposes for what is happening in the moment, we have a choice to make. Will we actively, intentionally, willingly cooperate with God's purpose (whatever it might be) or not? In the mid-seventeen hundreds, a French priest illustrated this idea in an interesting way:

> Is not a picture painted on the canvas by the application of one stroke of the brush at a time? Similarly the cruel chisel destroys a stone with each cut. But what the stone sufferers by repeated blows is no less than the shape the mason is making of it. And should a poor stone be asked, "What is happening to you?", it might reply, "Don't ask me. All I know is that for my part there is nothing for me to know or to do, only to remain steady under the hand of my master and to love him and suffer him to work out my destiny. It is for him to know how to achieve this. I know neither what he is doing nor why. I only know that he is doing what is best and most perfect, and I suffer each cut of the chisel as though it were the best thing

for me, even though, to tell the truth, each one is my idea of ruin, destruction, and defacement. But, ignoring all this, I rest contented with the present moment. Thinking only of my duty in it, I submit to the work of this skillful master without caring to know what it is."[14]

Of course, the illustration breaks down because the canvas and the stone have no choice – but we do. We can choose to cooperate with the master of our destiny or not; and we make these choices moment by moment, day by day, - for a lifetime. That same priest wrote:

…Everything that happens to us, in us, and through us, embraces and conceals God's divine but veiled purpose, so that we are always being taken by surprise and never recognize it until it is been accomplished. If we could pierce that veil and if we were vigilant and attentive, God would unceasingly reveal himself to us and we would rejoice in his works and in all that happens to us. We would say to everything: 'it is the Lord!' And we would discover that every circumstance is a gift from God; that human beings, frail creatures though they are, will never lack anything; and that God's unceasing concern is to give them what is best for them.[15]

There is a potential danger built into this way of thinking: just responding to all that happens in a passive way. In fact, the priest's English translator used the word 'passive' several times in the book. But, as you read the book, it becomes obvious that the kind of response the author is talking about is not at all what we think of when we hear the word 'passive'. This kind of spiritual surrender is not resignation. It is not choosing to quit caring. Nor is it Eastern mysticism – an attempt to get beyond the suffering of this life by going completely numb. Rather, the response that he recommends is active, intentional, willing, and cooperating with all that happens in our lives so that we can experience all the blessing and growth that God intends for us by allowing whatever it is to happen. Very often, we can only get a glimpse of the blessing and growth with twenty-twenty hindsight.

Dr. Tim Clinton recounts a story about a man held prisoner in a Russian gulag:

...When the prisoner was released, he walked through the gates to freedom and then turned and walked to the gray concrete wall. He bent down and kissed it. He said, "Thank you gulag. This is where I found God." Some of us have been in prison camps of abuse, heart ache, loneliness, and shame. When we can reframe our story like ... the Soviet prisoner, we too will thank God for the lessons we've learned through our suffering. ... Gradually, and with flashes of insight, we acknowledge that the lessons we learned through suffering are treasures to our hearts, we appreciate God's love far more than before, and we realize we have developed compassion for others who are hurting. We would never have chosen this path, but we've gained so much by walking it that we'd never choose any other.[16]

The bad things that happen in our lives can become 'treasures' in our lives when seen from the right perspective. When we recognize that bad things are really tokens of God's love for us, we receive another benefit that most of us would not think was possible: our physical brain is changed in a very special way. Dr. Timothy R. Jennings, is a Christian psychiatrist. He writes that, "The battlefield on which the war between Christ and Satan is fought is the mind."[17] He goes on to summarize recent brain research:

... Recent brain research by Dr. Newberg at the University of Pennsylvania has documented that all forms of contemplative meditation were associated with positive brain changes – but the greatest improvements occurred when participants meditated specifically on a God of love. Such meditation was associated with growth in the prefrontal cortex (the part of the brain right behind the forehead where we reason, make judgments, and experience Godlike love) and subsequent increased capacity for empathy, sympathy, compassion, and altruism. But here's the most astonishing part. Not only does other–centered love increase when we worship a God of love, but sharp thinking and memory improvement as well. In other words, worshiping a God of love actually stimulates the brain to heal and grow... choosing to operate in harmony with God's design results in better mental and physical health.[18]

"It is love that heals and restores, but genuine love is only experienced when the lies about God are removed."[19] In other words, Dr. Jennings believes that we can't experience genuine love until we're intentionally involved in the process of getting rid of strongholds, footholds, and memories that need healed. The apostle Peter wrote:

> Friends, when life gets really difficult, don't jump to the conclusion that God isn't on the job. Instead, be glad that you are in the thick of what Christ experienced. This is a spiritual refining process, with glory just around the corner.[20]

God loves us so much that He continues to work at deeper and deeper levels on those footholds, strongholds, and toxic memories that still need more healing. As C. S. Lewis said, God is going to go the 'whole way' if we will let Him. He is not just taking out the "bullet" that originally caused our wound. He then cleans out the wound to prevent infection and stitches it up, which sometimes hurts even more. Then, He bandages it, gives us spiritual and emotional medication, and redresses the wound until it is *completely* healed. Thank you Lord! As this healing takes place, we will feel better about ourselves and be happier as we get free, memories are healed, and, our brains are changed for the better. But these benefits must not be our primary focus. The benefits of knowing and walking with God are the result of our relationship with Jesus. Without that deep and growing relationship with Him, we may never learn to experience the true happiness, fulfillment, and joy that can be ours in the present and will fully be ours in heaven.[21]

We are involved in a continuing process of being healed and set free. It would be wonderful if we could just deal with something that is wrong in our life once and for all and never have to think about it again. Sometimes, that actually happens. Unfortunately, that is not the way things usually work. So, we must not let Satan discourage us because there may be more that needs to be worked on in our life. God reveals only what we need to deal with now. He won't overload us, overwhelm us, or discourage us by letting us see the full extent of our need or sinfulness all at once. As God reveals more, deal with that, and then, the next 'that' if there is one. Recognize God's continuing work in our lives for what it is: the proof of His unending love for us. Someone has given us an illustration of how this works: If you are carrying a lantern on a dark night and you hold it up in front of your face, you will be blinded and stumble. But, if you hold it down by your side, the pathway directly in front of you will be flooded with light. You will have enough light to take the next several steps safely. As you take those steps, both you and the light move forward. There will always be enough light for the next steps.

For example, God has been working on various parts of a 'controlling' problem in my life that has continued to surface in several different ways over a long time. I've described most of them earlier in this book. God helped me to see what was happening in my life one issue at a time. This seems to be the way God usually works. He started revealing Himself to mankind little by little beginning with the events recorded in Genesis and has continued revealing more and more ever since. The information and ideas for this book also came progressively, over time. God was both working on me and, at the same time, revealing more of what He wanted included in this book as it was being written. I will have to stop writing, sooner or later – but, the work in my own life will continue. Even though we know, almost certainly, that we will have to continue working on problems in our lives, we can still know happiness and joy and beauty and adventure because, in Jesus, we are "more than conquerors"[22]. This kind of life can be experienced in the present without indulging in the counterfeit self–fulfillment coming from our sinful desires. There is hope for *now,* and even greater hope for the future!

The events in our lives and in this world keep reminding us that we are living in a war zone. The 'bullets' are flying all around. The chances are pretty high that we are going to be hit again and again. If the devil gets his way, we will for sure. What matters is what we do when we get hit or when, in a flash of God-given insight, we recognize that we have been hit in the past and didn't realize it. When we were children, we often didn't have the resources to recognize our sin or process our toxic memories. As maturing Christians, we do. We can stay free if we will recognize and learn to use our resources.

One of the ways we can avoid being hit by one of the devil's bullets is to try to avoid those situations where it is more likely that we will be hit. For me, this means that I have to choose not to watch certain kinds of television programs or go to certain kinds of movies, for example, that will tempt me back into old patterns of thinking or behaving. Even as I am doing this, I need to be careful that I don't fall into another trap. It is the trap of "rule making and rule keeping". However well intentioned, rules (dos and don'ts) are not the best way for us stay free. Children may need rules, but those who are walking with God shouldn't need them. Knowing and doing the 'right' thing will come out of our relationship with God and be done as a natural consequence of 'who' we are – God's kids – kings and priests.[23] These right things will then be done in the power of the Holy Spirit. The danger is that we can begin to think that we can stay free and do the right things by our own efforts, our own determination, our own rules, our own discipline, our own giftedness, or a sense of obligation or duty. When we fail, we end up with guilt, shame, and depression. When we succeed, we end up with spiritual pride and a religious spirit. In the final analysis, we can stay free and avoid further damage in our lives only by learning and obeying God's truth - by replacing lies with truth, bondage with freedom, and toxic memories with memories that have been healed.

There is something else that is very important for us to consider as we continue our journey towards our goal of freedom from the lies and bondage of the one who wants to hurt God by hurting us. The real goal is not just *our* freedom. It is not just *about us - our* happiness, *our* joy, *our* fulfillment. So, what is the purpose of getting free? It is not just so *I* can get free. It is that, but also, so that each of us will be prepared to fulfill the purpose and destiny that God has prepared for us. We are simply not able to do this when our minds are filled with lies and we are in bondage to sin. What will these purposes and destinies be? It will be different for each person. But, it will involve helping to prepare God's people to do the work of the ministry that they each have been gifted and called to do. As we do this, others will be helped to become more like Jesus and then be able to help others they know to do the same[24]. Getting and staying free is a means to encourage God's destiny to be fulfilled in each of us and those God has placed us in relationship with. Eldredge writes:

> If we say we seek all of this for our own sake, we're right back where we started: lost in our own story. Jesus said that when a person lives merely to preserve his life, he eventually loses it all together. Rather, he said, "…give your life away and discover life as it was always meant to be. Self–help is no help at all. Self–sacrifice is the way, my way, to finding yourself,

your true self" (Matt. 16:25, *The Message*). Self–preservation, the theme of every small story, is so deeply wrong because it violates the Trinity, whose members live to bring glory *to the others*. The road we travel will take us into the battle to restore beauty in all things, chief among them the hearts of those we know. We grow in glory so that we might assist others in doing so; we give our glory to increase theirs. In order to fulfill the purpose of our journey, we need a passion to increase glory; we will need *love*.[25]

The phrase, 'to restore beauty in all things', reminds me of a vision that Rick Joyner writes about. In his vision, he saw a vast army moving across a great plane. There were twelve divisions that stood out sharply from the great multitude of soldiers who followed behind them. Joyner goes on to describe those in the front.

> Then I was close enough to see their faces – male and female, old and young from every race. There was a fierce resolution on their faces, yet they did not seem tense. War was in the air, but in the ranks I could sense such a profound peace that I knew that not a single one feared the battle to which they were marching. The spiritual atmosphere that I felt when close to them was as awesome as their appearance.... As I studied them, they seemed selfless – not because they lacked identity, but because they were all so sure of who they were and what they were doing. They were not consumed with themselves or seeking recognition. I could not detect ambition or pride anywhere in their ranks. It was stunning to see so many who were so unique, yet in such harmony and marching in perfect step. I was sure that there had never been an army on earth like this.... I was suddenly on a mountain where I could see the entire army. As I watched, I noticed that the plane was dry and dusty before the army, but immediately after the first 12 divisions past, the earth was dark green, with trees giving shade and bearing fruit and clear streams flowing throughout the land. This army was restoring the Earth. I thought how different this was from what would happen when one of the world's armies would pass through a land. They would plunder

and forage until the land was utterly stripped wherever they had marched.[26]

I read this description several years ago. But I still can remember clearly how much I wanted to be a part of that kind of army – renewing and restoring all that it passed over. I still want to be part of that kind of army. I hope and pray that you do too. God's work of renewal and restoration in us is not just about us. We are being healed and set free so that we can pass that same kind of healing and freedom on to others. But, first, we need to focus on getting ourselves involved in this long-term process. It's like using the oxygen masks that drop down in case of an emergency on a plane. We are instructed to care of ourselves first so that we can then help others around us. This sounds a lot like Jesus' instructions to us to take the plank out of our own eye before we try to take a speck out of someone else's eye.[27]

I know a wonderful, spiritually mature Christian woman who helps others gain the healing and freedom this book talks about. This is her story. She has given me permission to share it with you.

For ten years her husband Greg had suffered with depression, was fault-finding, negative and very angry. Then, at the age of 43, he had a major heart attack and bi-pass surgery. He was told that he could expect to live at least 20 years if he took care of himself. After that, he kept repeatedly saying, "I'm not going to live very long. I doubt that I'll live to be 50, then 60..." Three years after his heart attack, he and Mary went through Cleansing Stream training (learning to apply the resources described in this book and get free from bondage). Within two weeks, he experienced miraculous changes – the fault-finding, negativity, anger and depression were gone! All of a sudden he was full of joy and his heart turned toward the needs of other people. Life wasn't all about him anymore. His focus was changed from inward to outward. Both Greg and Mary began helping others find the freedom and spiritual blessings they had found.

Then, many years later, the depression came back. Greg refused to take the meds the doctor offered. He had been declining in health for several years but didn't take seriously his personal responsibility to do all he could to improve and care for his own health. Mary was all alone when, at the age of 62, Greg unexpectedly and very suddenly died.

Obviously, this was a very difficult and traumatic situation. She called 911 and tried to help him until the paramedics arrived. But, because of his physical size and unconscious state, there was little she could do to help. When these kinds of things happen to us, it matters very little how knowledgeable or spiritually mature we are. Satan will try to take advantage of any traumatic situation in our lives to hurt us in any way he can. In this case, Mary was hit with what she described as tsunami waves of guilt. "Why didn't I make him take better care of himself? If only I had … I should have … Why didn't I …? I should have been able to …" Even as she was going through all this, Mary had a sense that Jesus was right there with her. She knew she was not alone. In her mind's ear, she heard Jesus saying, "I'm here. You're okay, I'm here."

Early that morning, as she lay in her bed alone in the darkness crying, she heard herself singing *How Great Thou Art*. Mary recalls that, "As I sang it, every part of my being was in those words. I knew I was being held." In His greatness she received peace. In her mind's eye, Jesus took her right hand and said, "I've got you." Then, with her left hand, Mary grabbed onto His wrist and said, "And I've got You, and I'm not letting go!" Mary knew that everything was okay. It was all part of God's plan.

Mary has since re-lived those traumatic scenes several times but, "Every time there were those tsunami waves of grief, guilt, heartbreak, and sorrow. Every time, Jesus was there too. "Every time! I'd cry. I'd get to grieve a little while. But, then He'd pull me out of it and let me know its okay, and that I'm still here for a reason. I felt that I was immersed in an even bigger tsunami wave of God's love." She continued to have occasional bouts of guilt for almost a year. Then, she attended another Cleansing Stream retreat. At that event, the subject of 'Trauma' was covered. She received ministry to deal with the trauma related to Greg's death, and the traumatic effects from being the target of anger. After that, the waves of guilt and the 'video' replays of the death experience stopped.

Often now, her mind is filled with the music and words to two old hymns: *Great is Thy Faithfulness* and *It is well With My Soul*. *"When sorrows like sea billows roll, whatever my lot, He has taught me to say, it is well, it is well with my soul."* She said, "My soul would agree even though

I often sang it through tears. They were tears of sorrow but also tears of recognizing His loving Presence, His great compassion, and goodness."

This is an amazing example of 'contingent' experiences - having a real, vital, personal connection with Jesus, having Him respond to her in a way that was directly related to (contingent upon) what they were both experiencing and communicating. Mary also experienced 'attunement' with Jesus - the feeling that she and Jesus were both seeing, hearing, and understanding each other, that they cared about each other, and that they were glad to be together. This kind of relationship with Jesus is available to any of us who know and walk with Him.

It is so important how we choose to respond when bad things happen to us – when the 'nits' and the 'dragons' attack. We do have a choice. Mary responded one way. Greg responded another. Many of the things that happen to us *are* really beyond our control. We tend to give Satan too much credit for all that goes wrong. Our own behaviors, misunderstandings, and false conclusions about painful experiences are often the only initial cause. Then, evil spirits encourage and build on these wrong beliefs. So, strongholds and the resulting bondage (footholds) can initially come from sources other than evil spirits but can still be used by them to attack us. Someone has said that "God votes for us and Satan votes against us. We get to cast the deciding ballot." The ultimate purpose for all that goes on in our lives is to bring glory to God and to make us more like Jesus.[28] This is a process of *becoming*. The fruit God produces in us is for our benefit. But it is also for the benefit of others, to meet other's needs too. The focus is all about God and others. These ideas are found all throughout Scripture.

As life happens, there is a real potential for new strongholds to be established in our lives. These were, perhaps, more easily developed when we were young children, because, as children, we didn't personally have much influence on what we were exposed to. We were 'thought-sponges'. As adults, we can choose to fill our minds with God's truth so we can detect the 'toxins' of false teaching and wrong conclusions that we are constantly being exposed to. This is an on-going process that includes not just attending church but also, being faithful in our devotions and reading the Bible – especially the New Testament – and exposing ourselves to God's truth in its many forms.

It is still possible for strongholds to get established in our minds as adults. How can we keep strongholds from getting established or re-established in our lives? Sometimes we can't – simply because they can get established in our subconscious mind when we agree with something that is not truth when we experience the kind of traumatic things that can happen to us all. Even though this is true, there are things we can do to minimize the chances of further damage in our lives. The most important of these things is to continuously expose ourselves to God's truth. This kind of 'truth' is spiritually discerned truth which we finite human beings can understand only because God reveals it to us and then helps us understand it, as the Holy Spirit helps us as we deal with the nits and dragons. The ultimate source of God's truth is, of course, the Bible. But, because God is endlessly creative, there is a wide range of other ways God reveals His truth to us. We've discussed many of them in this book. Then, when the attack comes, we will have a better chance of recognizing the attack for what it is. We will have a better chance of coming through the experience stronger and wiser when we have intentionally exposed ourselves to God's truth.

George MacDonald wrote that "our God is an all-consuming fire that burns away all that is not eternal inside us." [29] In the context of this book, we are saying that the strongholds, footholds, hurtful memories, and sinful patterns of thinking (habits) need to be 'burned away' by God's truth. MacDonald also said that, those of us who can, will see that the 'burning' is actually *purification* and embrace it; but, that those who cannot see it as that, will see it as 'torture'. Those who willingly walk into God's purifying fire will experience the purification not as torture but simply as the light of truth.[30] I pray that you will continue to seek and embrace the light of God's truth. When we consciously expose ourselves to the light of God's truth, the lies in our thoughts will scurry away like cockroaches when a light is turned on–and be replaced by truth. The bondage potentially related to them will not get established in the first place.

Another way to stay free is to do everything we can to keep ourselves from forgetting the consequences of the lies we once believed and the pain we once encountered before we embraced the truth. Someone has said, "Our memory leaks." Don't let yourself forget. Remind yourself of truth that God has revealed you to in the past by rereading your journals every so often. If you haven't been journaling, start. If we don't journal, we *will* forget the special and precious things God has revealed to us. When we journal, we get multiple reinforcements of what we are writing down – we think it *and* we see it as we write it down. Even then, we still forget. Journaling is making it possible to be reminded later – It is 'preparing to remember'. Journaling is not just a diary. It is a written record of our thoughts, our struggles, our insights, our ideas, our questions that we want God to answer or that He has already answered, our recognized strongholds and the truth statements God personally gave us to replace them - all this and more. Our journals are a record of our walk with God. Make and keep that record. It is a priceless treasure. It is your own 'story'. And, it is never too late to start.

Eldredge has written that, "*How* we remember is as important as *what* we remember."[31] His point is that we tend to get exposed to God's truth primarily through the learning of Biblical facts, doctrinal information about who God is, about the things He has revealed to us in the Bible, and about facts that He wants us to *understand.* This is especially true in our western Christian culture. We are an 'information-based', 'knowledge-based' culture. These are good things to know and to understand. But, if we stop with knowledge *about* God, we have not exposed ourselves to the whole truth, the 'truth' that includes experiencing God Himself. Yes, we do need to learn propositional truth and facts – but, we also need stories that illustrate them. Stories 'bring to life' the application of truth. Stories help us understand the realities within the doctrines and other facts we have learned. Stories show us real-life as it is lived out day by day. Stories tell us how others have dealt with the nits and the dragons. Stories are often gritty and, yet, beautiful - stories like Greg's and Mary's story. Eldredge says it this way:

> Satan will do everything he can to steal the romance [the love-story that *is* Jesus]. One way he does this is to leave us only propositions, or worse "principles," like "the management techniques of Jesus" or "the marketing methods of Jesus." The heart cannot live on facts and principles alone; it speaks the language of story and we must rehearse the truths of our faith in a way that captures the heart and not just the mind.[32]

C. S. Lewis gives us another way to think about the growth in our understanding of truth that will help us stay free. It is a way of understanding truth that Lewis calls 'transposition'.[33] We usually try to explain something to someone who has never experienced it by using language or illustrations that are part of what they *have* previously experienced. God uses this kind of language and explanation in the Bible to help us understand spiritual truth that we otherwise couldn't understand. Understanding new truth always requires God's revelation of the new truth to us in ways we can understand by using things familiar to us in our present, limited, space-time existence. The new truth will never contradict, change, or replace the truth or reality of our earlier (Biblically based) understandings. It will, however, build on and incorporate the new truth into our earlier understandings. So, as we grow in our walk with God and continue to expose ourselves to His truth, we will begin to understand additional spiritual truth that we couldn't understand before. God progressively reveals more and more truth to us as we become able to receive it. When we do understand additional truth, we need to be careful not to fall into the trap of becoming spiritually prideful. And, alternatively, when we have difficulty understanding some specific spiritual truth, we need to be careful that we don't fall into the trap of being unnecessarily critical of ourselves. We need to simply recognize that we are having difficulty understanding a particular spiritual truth right now. It may be that we are just not *ready* to understand it *yet*. Give it time. Stick with it. God will give us the ability to understand what we need to understand when we need to understand it. This applies, of course, to recognizing our strongholds, footholds, and toxic memories as well as to our understanding of more and more Biblical truth. We need to stay in this process even though we don't know what new understanding or insight will surface next or what new problem we will have to deal with.

One of the problems we all have to deal with is our tendency to 'buy into' the thinking and behavioral patterns that our culture and demonic influence tries to lead us into. When we do, we establish strongholds, footholds, and have hurtful experiences. We also develop sinful and destructive *habits* of thinking and behaving that also need to be replaced. In a way, habits of thinking are like 'thought-addictions'. These habits are a set of behaviors and ways of thinking that have been established by our *own* repeated, long-term, *personal* cooperation with cultural and satanic influence. This is true whether we consciously recognized it or not as it was happening. A sinful habit, just like a good habit, is part of *us* (our deeply integrated biological brain and spiritual soul). It is not a lie (stronghold) we can replace with truth or a separate spiritual entity, a demonic influence (foothold) we can choose to break using God's authority and power. It is a part of *us* that *we* need to deal with. This is almost always a lot easier to say than to do because it is up to *us* to do it – using the resources God has provided. If what these resources are don't immediately come to mind, I suggest you go back and carefully reread chapter three.

We are all aware of how much easier it is to sin in a particular way once we have begun to sin repeatedly in that area – once we have established a sinful habit. Even though we have replaced the lies with truth and the demonic bondages have been broken, the habits of sinful behavior related to them will usually still be there. We find ourselves behaving in sinful ways without even thinking about it. The difference now, though, is that thinking and behaving in Godly ways will be much easier because we won't have the unrecognized lies and demonically driven compulsion coming from the related footholds. The Bible says that, when we resist the devil, he will flee from us.[34] We also need to consistently resist sinful habits. But, doing so requires focused, concentrated, long-term effort on our part. Someone has said that it takes a continuing effort for 28 days to break a habit. For me, it *feels* like it takes even longer. Over time, the habits will be broken and, most of the time, even the temptation to sin in that same way will no longer be as strong. If we refuse to make the effort necessary to break sinful habits, we will re-establish the footholds we have broken, end up right back in bondage, and have to start all over again. When this happens, we can become trapped in a vicious cycle; trapped in a 'prison of despair', experiencing shame and guilt; losing hope and weighed down by repeated failure. We are told that one way to break a bad habit is to replace it with a good habit. This strategy is strongly supported by Scripture. Many people habitually worry and are anxious, for example. The Bible tells us to pray about whatever we are worrying or anxious about and God will give us 'peace that passes understanding'. The very next verse then tells us to replace the worry by thinking about good stuff – things that are true, noble, right, pure, lovely, admirable, excellent, and praiseworthy.[35]

We learned earlier in this chapter that, when we think about a God of love and behave in loving ways, our brains are changed in a very positive way. Dr, Jennings has documented that the opposite is also true. When we think about wrong and fearful things and behave in sinful ways, our brains are changed too, but, in very negative ways. He explains in medical terms exactly how this happens. And then he puts it in terms those of us who are not medical doctors can understand. He says that the part of our brain that we use is encouraged to grow and the part we don't use is "pruned". The parts of our brains that are active are fed the equivalent of biological 'fertilizer' and grow stronger. The parts of our brains that are inactive get the equivalent of biological 'weed killer' and die. In this case as well as many others, the old saying 'use it or lose it' is literally true. "The thoughts we think actually reshape our brains!"[36] As C. S. Lewis and others have said, we progressively become 'beings we might be tempted to worship' or 'nightmarish creatures'. We do this one thought, one decision, and one behavior at a time. We are all like caterpillars in a chrysalis. We are progressively being transformed into something else; some into beautiful butterflies, some into monsters. We need to be *really* careful about the kinds of things we let our brains think about and the things we choose to do if we want strong, healthy brains. Of course, the Bible tells us to do the same thing:

We demolish arguments and every pretension that sets itself up against the knowledge of God, and we take captive every thought to make it obedient to Christ.[37]

Dr. Jennings puts it this way:

Why must we bring every thought into captivity to Jesus? Because, if we don't actively stop firing unhealthy neural circuits, those unhealthy thought patterns will not degrade and our characters will not be transformed into Christ's likeness. This is the meaning behind Jesus' famous interpretation of adultery: "You have heard that it was said, 'you shall not commit adultery.' But I tell you that anyone who looks at a woman lustfully has already committed adultery with her in his heart" (Matthew 5:27–28. Jesus knew, of course that, if we continue to commit sin in our imaginations, those unhealthy circuits grow stronger and our characters cannot be healed. One Bible writer says, in the old King James Version, "For as he thinketh in his heart, so is he" (Proverbs 23:7). The decisions we make in our hearts determine which neural circuits get fired, either in action or in imagination. But either way, it is the neural circuits the heart chooses that get activated and thus strengthened and retrained.[38]

When we recognize that God truly loves us and that even the nits and dragons are used by Him for our highest good; when we intentionally expose ourselves to God's truth; when we do things for the right reasons and focus on helping others; when we seek contingent communication and attunement with Jesus; when we focus on meanings and understanding rather than rules and principals; when we journal so that we can be reminded of God's work in our lives; when we establish relationships with people of loving and mature character, and terminate destructive and exploitative relationships in our lives; when we maintain regular devotional times; when we refuse to think thoughts that 'set themselves up against the knowledge of God'; when we intentionally work at breaking destructive habit patterns of thought and behavior; the parts of our brains that think these kinds of thoughts and support these kinds of actions grow stronger. When we think thoughts and do things that help us get rid of strongholds, footholds, and toxic memories, we get better and better at doing it because our biological brain actually changes in ways that helps us do it more consistently and more effectively. As we do this consistently, we build good habits rather than bad ones. Our brains have been designed to function in ways that are even better than we ever imagined. If this isn't good news, I don't know what is!

Jack Hayford summarizes the Christian's relationship to suffering:

The Bible teaches that suffering, trial, and all order of human difficulty are unavoidable; but God's Word teaches us that they all may be overcome. The presence of the King and the power of His Kingdom in our lives make us neither invulnerable nor immune to life's struggles. But they do bring the promise of victory: provision in need, strength for the day, and healing, comfort, and saving help.[39]

A daily devotional that is written as though Jesus were speaking to us personally says it this way:

> Beloved, I know how difficult it is for you control of your thoughts. Your mind is a battleground, and the evil spirits work tirelessly to influence your thinking: even deceiving you with intrusive thoughts at times. Your own selfishness also finds ample expression in your thoughts. You need to stay alert in the fight against evil! I fought and died for you, so remember who you are and *Whose* you are. Thus, you put on the helmet of salvation. This helmet not only protects your mind, it also reminds you of the victory I secured for you on the cross. Your thoughts are precious to me because you are my treasure. As soon as your thinking turns my way, I notice and rejoice. The more thoughts you bring to me, the more you can share in my joy. I disarm evil thoughts and render them powerless. Then I help you think thoughts about things that are true, noble, right, pure, lovely, admirable – excellent and praiseworthy things. Ponder these things, while resting in the peace of my presence.[40]

During the last meal Jesus and His disciples would eat together here on earth, He said, "I don't have much more time to talk to you, for the evil prince of this world approaches. He has no power over me."[41] The word Jesus used for 'power' is the same word translated as 'foothold' in Ephesians 4:26. When we sin, we establish a foothold. Jesus was saying that Satan had no power over Him because He was sinless. *No sin means no foothold.* When we are tempted to think thoughts that are sinful, we are actually being tempted to establish footholds. Every wrong action is preceded by a wrong thought. The only way to avoid establishing footholds is to 'take thoughts captive' so that they can't lead us into bondage (footholds). Simply refuse to entertain thoughts or imaginations that will lead to more sinful thoughts and, eventually, to sinful behaviors. How do we do that? When we recognize a sinful thought for what it is, we then use the power and authority we have already been given by Jesus to interrupt the thought and say to any evil spirit that might be able to hear you (and to your own sin nature at the same time) something like this:

Spirit of… (lust, anger, fear…) you get out of my mind right now in Jesus name! I refuse to think your thoughts.

That is all there is to it. We don't have to say it loudly but we do need to say it verbally and really mean it. Remember, evil spirits can't read our unspoken thoughts. Then, we intentionally direct our thoughts to 'good stuff'. Recall a favorite Bible verse. Sing a favorite hymn or song. Pray. Whatever. Just don't leave your mind empty without something good of your own choosing to think about. *You* decide what you will think about, guided by the Holy Spirit. Don't allow your thoughts to be controlled or influenced by anything except your own spiritually informed choices. Obviously, this is hard to do consistently. But, with practice and persistence, it can be done most of the time. C.S. Lewis said,

> One can't help momentary [sinful thoughts]; guilt begins only when one embraces them. You can't help their knocking at the door, but you mustn't ask them in to lunch.[42]

Footholds are established only when we 'embrace' wrong thoughts; when we make agreements with them; when we 'invite them in to lunch'; allow them to stay in our minds. Just tell your sinful thoughts (through the closed door) to go away and to get off your property.

The Bible says that we have no obligation whatever to our old sin nature to do what it begs us to do.[43] The same is also true about temptations or suggested thoughts from any evil spirit. The thoughts we have can come from our own minds; they can come from the devil; they can come from God; or, they can come from these same sources through others. If a thought is even 'questionable', all we have to do is compare it with what we know of God's truth. Godly thoughts will never contradict what has already been given us in the Bible. If it is a Godly thought, think about it; expand on it; turn it over in your mind; agree with it. If it is not a Godly thought, reject it. It is up to us to choose. Remember, God votes for us, the devil votes against us and we get to cast the deciding ballot. Charles Spurgeon wrote:

> The utmost consecration of spirit will not ensure you against satanic temptation. Christ was consecrated through and through. It was His meat and drink to do the will of Him that sent Him: and yet He was tempted! Your hearts may glow with the seraphic flame of love to Jesus and yet the devil will

still try to bring you down… If you will tell me when God permits Christians to lay aside their armor, I will tell you when Satan has given up temptation. Like the old knights in times of battle, we must sleep with the helmet and breastplate buckled on, for the arch–deceiver will seize our first unguarded hour to make us his prey.[44]

When we realize that we have entertained ungodly thoughts rather than rejecting them, all we have to do is to give our minds a spiritual 'bath' by confessing our sinful thinking.[45] The Apostle Paul tells us to:

> … Throw off your old evil nature – the old one that was a partner in your evil ways – rotten through and through, full of lust and sham. Now your attitudes and thoughts must all be constantly changing for the better. Yes you must be a new and different person, holy and good. Clothe yourself with this new nature.[46] …I plead with you to give your bodies to God. Let them be a holy and living sacrifice – the kind He will accept. When you think of what He has done for you, is this too much to ask? Don't copy the behavior and customs of this world, but let God transform you by changing the way you think. Then you will know what God wants you to do and you will know how good and pleasing and perfect His will really is.$

It is our choice to make. God has paid the price of our sin (death) and has chosen to love us. Will we choose to love Him back by believing Him and doing what He says? The daily devotional I quoted from above expresses these thoughts in the following words from Jesus:

> Beloved, I created you in My image: with the capacity to communicate with Me. As My image-bearer, you have the ability to choose the focus of your mind. I understand that many thoughts come and go unbidden, but you can control your thinking more than you realize. Under the inspiration of the Holy Spirit, Paul wrote, "Whatever is true, whatever is noble, whatever is right… think about such things." I would not instruct you to think about certain things unless it was possible to do so. Because the world contains both good and evil, you can choose to think about excellent, praiseworthy things or about terrible, upsetting things. Sometimes, of course, you

have to deal with the brokenness around you. However, each day contains moments when you are free to choose the focal point of your mind. These are the times when I want you to take charge of your thoughts. When your mind is idle, it often moves toward a negative focus – such as regretting things in your past or worrying about the future. Meanwhile, I am with you in the present: waiting for you to recall My Presence. Train your mind to turn toward Me frequently. Remembrance of who I am can brighten even your darkest times, blessing you with Joy.[48]

None of us has completely done all that we know to do perfectly. None of us ever will this side of heaven. We are in the training process of becoming more and more like Jesus. C. S. Lewis put it this way:

After each failure, ask forgiveness, pick yourself up, and try again. Very often what God first helps us toward is not the virtue itself but just the power of always trying again. For however important chastity (or courage, or truthfulness, or any other virtue) maybe, this process trains us in habits of the soul which are more important still. It cures our illusions about ourselves and teaches us to depend on God. We learn, on the one hand, that we cannot trust ourselves even in our best moments and, on the other, that we need not despair even in our worst, for our failures are forgiven. The only fatal thing is to sit down content with anything less than perfection.[49]

The Bible is filled with examples of those who did the things we have been talking about and, also, about those who didn't. In either case, they experienced the inevitable consequences of what they thought and did. We are told, for example about King David. He, like most of us, is an example of doing both good and bad.

King David experienced many kinds of trials during his life and he did something that is worth noting: *he encouraged himself* in the Lord. The Psalms are full of this kind of 'encouragement'. David sought encouragement and strength from the Lord. He went to the one who held the final word over his difficult situation. We can do this too. We can find strength from the Lord through His Word and in the words we speak to ourselves during painful or depressing circumstances. Consider these passages: Psalm 18:1–2, Psalm 43:3–4, Psalm 141:8–9…[50]

We have thought together about the things that will help us stay free. One thing remains that is just as important as all the others. It is persistence, hanging in there, 'keeping on keeping on'. We need to make a commitment to keep doing the things we can do to help us on our journey. The process of getting free and staying free is like taking a long hike. If we are going to reach our goal, we are going to have to just keep putting one foot in front of the other. When life is pleasant it is easier than when life is terrible. But it is all part of the journey. We are running a marathon – not a 100 yard dash. We are told that long distance runners sometimes feel that they have 'hit a wall', have run out of steam, and just can't go any farther. In our Christian walk with God, we sometimes feel like we have 'hit a wall'. Some Marathon runners manage to just keep going even when they 'hit the wall'. Pure discipline? Pure habit? Christians have an additional resource. We are not 'running' in our own strength. The Bible says:

> … continue to work out your salvation with fear and trembling, for it is God who works in you to will and to do and to act according to his good purpose.[51] …not by might nor by power, but by my Spirit,' says the Lord Almighty.[52]

Once we are strong and healthy, then, we need to learn how to stay that way. Physically, we can do that through eating a balanced diet, getting regular sleep, drinking plenty of water, exercising the mind and body regularly, avoiding toxins, and staying away from things or activities that we know have a high probability of hurting us. As we do this we will get stronger and healthier than we would otherwise be. Spiritually, we need to keep repeating the things we've discussed above as often as needed. All children fall back on their diapers often as they learn to walk. We don't get angry with them; rather, we praise them for continuing to try. Someone has said that, '*real* failure is not trying and failing, but, refusing to try.' God is pleased with us when we keep trying. As long as there is even one stronghold, foothold, or toxic memory left, there is the potential for Satan to entrap us back in to his network of lies and bondage. It is like being on a diet, if we drift back into our old eating habits, we'll drift back into our old weight. Just keep thinking and doing what we know we need to be thinking and doing. And, wonder of wonders, God has created our brains so that, as we consistently do these things, our brain changes in ways that will help us continue! Jesus tells us to:

> Be very careful, then, how you live – not as unwise but as wise, making the most of every opportunity, because the days are evil.[53] I have told you these things, so that in me you may have peace. In this world, you will have trouble. But take heart! I have overcome the world.[54]

> As we continue to do this, we will continue to grow and get stronger in our walk with God. This growth and strength will happen little by little. When Israel entered the promised land, God said,

> Little by little I will drive them out before you, until you have increased enough to take possession of the land.[55]

Sometimes, our growth seems maddingly slow or even reversing. God loves us too much to give us more than we can handle sooner than we can handle it. Getting too much, too fast can result in overconfidence or spiritual pride. When we get overconfident and spiritually proud, we have believed a lie that we can handle more than we can (we have established another stronghold) and we have given a place of influence (a foothold) back to evil spirits. When that happens, we're back in trouble again! But, now we know what to do to get our freedom back.

There is a great danger built into the process of becoming and staying free. It is the danger we just mentioned above: spiritual pride. After we have been successfully freed from the bondage of the most obvious footholds, after we have recognized several strongholds and replaced them with truth, after we have had several hurtful memories healed, we will be tempted to believe that we are somehow special, closer to God than others, and have some special knowledge or ability that others don't. These beliefs are the kinds of *new* strongholds that Satan will try to establish in our minds as we are truly making real progress in our walk with God. Gerald May refers to this danger as 'spiritual narcissism'. He writes:

At this point it becomes relatively easy to understand how many people become excessively self–concerned and self–important after having undergone strong spiritual experiences; how some "leaders" begin in an attitude of humble service and wind up as megalomaniacs; and how certain spiritual groups begin with simple shared and supportive experience and wind up as rigidly exclusive, strongly self–propounding cults. This is the ultimate skulduggery of ego, spiritual narcissism in full bloom. In my opinion it is the greatest pitfall that spiritual seekers encounter; we have never known one who has managed to avoid it entirely, and I have known many who have spent months and even years in its tentacles.[56]

The truth is that there is absolutely no basis for spiritual pride since the only thing we can do that has any eternal value is what we allow the Holy Spirit to do through us. And, even that 'allowing' is not something that we can take credit for since 'it is God Who works in us to will and to do'[57]. Timothy Keller puts it this way:

> In Christ I could know that I was accepted by grace not only despite my flaws, but because I was willing to admit them. The Christian gospel is that I am so flawed that Jesus had to die for me, yet I am so loved and valued that Jesus was glad to die for me. This leads to deep humility and deep confidence at the same time. It undermines both swaggering and sniveling. I cannot feel superior to anyone, and yet I have nothing to prove to anyone. I do not think more of myself nor less of myself. Instead, I think of myself less. I don't need to notice myself – how I'm doing, how I'm being regarded – so often.[58]

When we find ourselves back in trouble again, or even when we think we're doing well in our walk with God, we will always be more successful in the context of relationship with others – a mentor, a life coach, a counselor, a friend, a small group... to encourage us and help us when we need it. Just as different doctors specialize in different areas of medical or psychological help, sometimes we need to seek out someone who specializes in providing special kinds of spiritual help too. Someone has said that, 'if the only tool in your toolbox is a hammer, then everything looks like a nail.' A hammer isn't of much use if you really need to drill a small hole. So, when you need help, get the kind of help you need from the best source available to you. Of course this encouragement and help goes both ways. We've all heard the saying, 'the best ability is availability.' This nugget of 'wisdom' is simply not true in every circumstance. If you know how to help someone, by all means, do it. If not, then help them find someone who does know how to help. We need to be ready to encourage and help others in every way we can. Sometimes, that means pointing them to someone else.

When Jesus sets us free, we keep getting progressively freer. We get free from strongholds, from footholds, and from memories with toxic content. We get free from all the things that limit our fellowship with God and our use of the resources He has given us. When Jesus sets us free, we are **free, free, free!** Let's do everything we possibly can to stay that way.

Chapter 8 After Word

A personal word from the author:

In this book, God has been helping us reach past the purely intellectual understanding of our biological minds to gain greater spiritual understanding. We have been encouraging our soul and spirit to rise up in the power of the Holy Spirit and exert His delegated power and authority in Jesus' name over all the power and influence of evil forces. We've been encouraged to see that there is more to reality than we thought there was. Just a few years ago, scientists thought that they were seeing all there was to see as they looked at the heavens with their marvelous satellites and telescopes and at sub-particle matter with their electron microscopes and particle accelerators. They have even been able to look back in time and see the light from nearly the beginning of space-time as the first stars were being born. They have since discovered that they were seeing less than five percent of what was really there - either in the very large or in the very small. There is also more to spiritual reality than we think there is. God is graciously revealing to us that we have only seen a small part of all he wants us to see. Once the eternal is recognized (even if we know we can only see a tiny part of it), the temporary can be transformed as it is seen in the light of eternal reality. The temporary things we see can be like scary shadows in a child's room at night. When the light is turned on, they are seen for what they really are. Evil forces are among the temporary things. May God grant us the courage and grace to open our spiritual eyes, discover progressively more and more of God's reality, and allow Him to do His wonderful transforming work in us. Strongholds, footholds, and toxic memories are barriers that hinder our relationship with God and others. As we cooperate with God in getting rid of them, we are progressively transformed – embracing more and more of God's truth and becoming more and more like Jesus.

This book was published as an outreach of 'Luke 4:18 Ministries', a religious, not-for-profit corporation. I would love to hear how this book has impacted your life or the life of someone you know personally. Has it raised questions in your mind that you would like to have answers for? Are there things said in the book that you feel weren't clear or, perhaps, that you feel are wrong? Are there subjects that you wish I had covered or had covered in greater detail? Would you like to personally discuss these truths with someone in your area who understands these truths and is experienced in helping others find freedom? I encourage you to visit the website: Luke4-18Ministries.org. You can email me at Don@luke4-18Ministries.org.

If you are a prayer warrior, I invite you to pray regularly for God's continued blessing to be on this ministry. I pray daily for God's blessing and the continuing revelation of His truth for all those who read this book.

I believe that this book provides information, guidance, and insights that are desperately needed by the greater Christian community. I want to see it have the widest distribution possible. If you agree, please recommend it to your friends or, maybe, even give them a copy. Additional copies of this book are available (or can be ordered) through your local Christian bookstore, purchased at Amazon.com, or through the Luke4-18Ministries website.

If you are a Christian pastor, life-coach, counselor, or therapist who would like to join a network of Christian 'helpers' who have personally experienced the truths discussed in this book, and you are available to help others to experience the freedom available to them, please contact me.

The abundant life that Jesus came to give us[1] includes finding ourselves immersed in the eternal giving and receiving of other-centered *agape* love with the triune God and His other loving creatures[2]. This can be experienced to a greater and greater degree, increasing unimaginably, as we become more and more free from strongholds, footholds, and hurtful memories. I challenge you to experience this abundant life for yourself. Remember, God votes for you. Satan votes against you. You get to cast the deciding ballot.

"And this same God who takes care of me will supply all your needs from his glorious riches, which have been given to us in Christ Jesus."[3]

Yours always in Him,

Don Stewart

APPENDIX A

Recommended Reading and Other Resources

The Trustworthiness of the Bible/Biblical Apologetics:

1. C. S. Lewis, *The Weight of Glory*, (New York, NY, Harper Collins Publishers,1976)

2. C. S. Lewis, *Meer Christianity*, (New York, NY: Simon & Schuster, Inc., 1980)

3. J. B. Phillips, *Ring Of Truth*,(Wheaton, IL, Harold Shaw Publishers, 1967)

4. Norman Geisler and Paul Hoffman, eds. *Why I Am A Christian: Leading Christians Explain Why They Believe*, (Grand Rapids, MI: Baker Publ. Group, 2001). Very good contributions overall by top-notch scholars, such as William Lane Craig, Gary Habermas, and Hugh Ross, on a variety of standard apologetic topics.

5. Norman L. Geisler, *Baker Encyclopedia of Christian Apologetics*, (Grand Rapids, MI, Baker Books, 1999)

6. Josh McDowell, *Evidence for Christianity*. (Nashville, TN: Nelson Reference & Electronic, 2006). This is a treasury of apologetics resources from one of the most influential and effective Christian apologists of the last four decades.

7. C. S. Lewis, *God in the Dock*, edited by Walter Hooper, (Grand Rapids, MI, Eerdmans Publishing Company, 1970)

8. Dan Story, *Defending Your Faith: Reliable Answers For A New Generation Of Seekers and Skeptics*, (Grand Rapids, MI, Kregel Publications, 1997)

9. *The Truth Project*, DVD set, Available from: www.thetruthproject.org. This is a small group training program originally from Focus on the Family.

10. Timothy Keller, *The Reason for God: Belief in a Age of Skepticism*, (New York, NY, Dutton, 2008). A down-to-earth and brilliant proof for the existence of God.

11. Kenneth Richard Samples, *Without a Doubt, Answering the 20 Toughest Faith Questions*, (Grand Rapids, MI, Baker Publishing Group, 2004)

Science and Creation:

1. Hugh Ross, *Hidden Treasures in the Book of Job: Answers to today's Scientific Questions*, (Grand Rapids, MI, Baker Books, 2011)

2. Hugh Ross, *Why is the Universe the Way it Is*, (Grand Rapids, MI, Baker Books, 2008)

3. Hugh Ross, *More Than A Theory: Revealing a Testable Model for Creation*, (Grand Rapids, MI, Baker Books, 2009)

4. Hugh Ross, *The Creator and the Cosmos: How the Latest Scientific Discoveries Reveal God*, (Colorado Springs, CO, NavPress, 1993)

5. Hugh Ross, *Who Was Adam?: A Creation Model For The Origin of Man*, (Colorado Springs, CO, NavPress, 2005)

6. Hugh Ross, *Creation and Time: A Biblical and Scientific Perspective on the Creation-Date Controversy*, (Colorado Springs, CO, NavPress, 1994)

7. Hugh Ross, *The Genesis Question: Scientific Advances and the Accuracy of Genesis*, (Colorado Springs, CO, NavPress, 1998)

8. J. Ligon Duncan III, David W. Hall, Hugh Ross and Gleason L. Archer, *The Genesis Debate: Three Views on the Days of Creation*, (Colorado Springs, CO, NavPress, 2001)

Spiritual Gifts:

1. Jerry Cook, *The Holy Spirit: So…What's The Big Deal*, (North Charleston, SC, CreateSpace Independent Publishing Platform, 2013)

2. Example of the prophetic gift: Rick Joyner, *The Call*, (Charlotte, NC, Morning Star Publications, 1999), and also, Rick Joyner, *A Prophetic vision for the 21st Century: A Spiritual Map to Help You Navigate into the Future*, (Nashville, TN: Thomas Nelson, Inc., 2004). Both of these books are well worth reading.

3. Guy P. Duffield and Nathaniel M. Van Cleave, Foundations of Pentecostal Theology, (San Dimas, CA, Life Bible College, 1983), 326-356

Biblical Truth and Discipleship:

1. J. I. Packer, *Knowing God*, (Downers Grove, IL, InterVarsity Press, 1973)

2. C. S. Lewis, *Meer Christianity*, (New York, NY: Simon & Schuster, Inc., 1980)

3. C. S. Lewis, *The Weight of Glory*, (New York, NY, Harper Collins Publishers,1976) John Eldredge, Utter *Relief of Holiness: How God's Goodness Frees Us from Everything that Plagues Us,*(New York, NY, FaithWorks Hachette Book Group, 2013)

4. Kenneth Richard Samples, *7 Truths That Changed The World*, (Grand Rapids, MI, Baker Publishing Group, 2012)

5. Kenneth Richard Samples, *A World of Difference , Putting Christian Truth-claims to the Worldview Test*, (Grand Rapids, MI, Baker Publishing Group, 2007)

6. C. S. Lewis, *The Joyful Christian*, (New York, N.Y.. Macmillan Publishing Company, Inc., 1977)

7. Dr. Dan B. Allender and Dr. Tremper Longman III, *Bold Love*, (Colorado Springs, CO, NavPress,1992)

8. John Eldredge, *The Sacred Romance*, (Nashville, TN: Thomas Nelson, Inc., 2004)

9. John Eldredge, *Waking The Dead*, (Nashville, TN: Thomas Nelson, Inc., 2003)

10. John Eldredge, Walking With God, (Nashville, TN: Thomas Nelson, Inc., 2008)

11. John Eldredge, *Beautiful Outlaw*, (New York, N.Y., FaithWords Hachette Book Group, 2011)

12. John Eldredge, *The Journey of Desire: Searching For The Life We've Only Dreamed Of*, (Nashville, TN: Thomas Nelson, Inc., 2002)

13. Brennan Manning, *Ruthless Trust: The Ragamuffin's Path to God*, (New York, NY, Harper Collins Publishers,2000)

14. Dallas Willard, *The Devine Conspiracy: Discovering Our Hidden Life In God*, (New York, NY, HarperCollins Publishers, 1997)

15. John Bevere, *The Bait of Satan: Your Response Determines Your Future*, (Lake Mary, FL, Creation House, 1994)

16. Tim Lahaye, *Revelation Unveiled*, (Grand Rapids, MI, Zondervan, 1999)

17. C. S. Lewis, *The Four Loves*, (London, Harcourt, Inc.,1960)

18. C. S. Lewis, *God in the Dock*, edited by Walter Hooper, (Grand Rapids, MI, Eerdmans Publishing Company, 1970)

19. Brennan Manning, *A Glimpse Of Jesus: The Stranger To Self-Hatred*, (New York, NY, HarperCollins Publishers, 2003)

20. Thomas V. Morris, *Making Sense of It All: Pascal and the Meaning Of Life*, (Grand Rapids, MI, Eerdmans Publishing Company, 1992)

21. *The Truth Project*, DVD set, Available from: www.Thetruthproject.org.

22. Douglas R. Groothuis, *Christian Apologetics: A Comprehensive Case for Biblical Faith*, (Downers Grove, IL, InterVarsity Press, 2011)

23. Ted Cabal, General Editor, *The Apologetics Study Bible: Real Questions, Straight Answers, Stronger Faith*, (Nashville, TN: Holman Bible Publishers, 2007)

24. Bible Study, available from www.jerichoventures.com

25. Larry Osborne, *10 Dumb Things Smart Christians Believe*, (Colorado Springs, CO: Multnomah Books, 2009)

26. John Bevere, *Under Cover: The Promise of Protection Under His Authority*, (Nashville, TN: Thomas Nelson, Inc., 2001)

27. Dallas Willard, *The spirit of the Disciplines: Understanding How God Changes Lives*, (San Francisco, CA, HarperSanFrancisco, 1991)

28. C. Baxter Kruger, Ph. D., *The Shack Revisited*, (New York, NY FaithWords, 2012)

29. Jack W. Hayford, *The Hayford Bible Handbook*, (Nashville, TN: Thomas Nelson, Inc., 1995)

Healing Memories:

1. Karl Lehman, M.D., *Outsmarting Yourself: Catching Your Past Invading The Present And What to Do About It*,(Libertyville, IL, This JOY! Books, 2011)

2. David Seamands, *Healing of Memories*, (Colorado Springs, CO, Chariot Victor Publishing, 1985)

3. Gregory A. Boyd and Al Larson, *Escaping the Matrix, Setting Your Mind Free to Experience Real Life in Christ*, (Grand Rapids, MI, Baker Publishing Group, 2005)

4. Chester and Betsy Kylstra, *Biblical Healing and Deliverance: A Guide To Experiencing Freedom*, (Grand Rapids, MI, Baker Publishing Group, 2005)

How Our Mind Works/Personality/Vision/Life Purpose:

1. Karl Lehman, M.D., *Outsmarting Yourself: Catching Your Past Invading The Present And What to Do About It*,(Libertyville, IL, This JOY! Books, 2011)

2. Dr. Tim Clinton and Dr. Joshua Straub, *God Attachment: Why You Believe, Act, and Feel The Way You Do About God*, (New York, NY, Howard Books, 2010)

3. Timothy R. Jennings, M.D., *The God-Shaped Brain: How Changing Your View Of God Transforms Your Life*, (Downers Grove, IL, InterVarsity Press, 2013)

4. David Keirsey and Marilyn Bates, *Please Understand Me: Character & Temperament Types*, (Del Mar, CA, Prometheus Nemesis Books, 1978)

5. For help with an evaluation of your values, purpose, and goals, visit www.chazown.com. Self evaluation is free.

6. *Brain Resources*, and *Living Animation*, available free from www.jerichoventures.com

7. .Dr. Tim Clinton & Dr. Gary Sibcy, *Attachments: Why You Love, Feel and Act the Way You Do,* (Brentwood, TN, Thomas Nelson Publishers, 2002). Attachment styles are a systematic way of describing a particular set of related beliefs about yourself and others. To the extent that these beliefs are not true, they are strongholds. As you read this book, you will discover your own attachment style. You may discover that many of the things you have believed are not really true and have been hiding in your unconscious mind. It might even feel like the authors have been videotaping your life. Reading books like this one and the others listed can reveal previously unrecognized strongholds so you can begin the process of replacing them with truth and getting memories healed.

Daily Devotionals:

1. Charles Haddon Spurgeon, *Morning and Evening: Daily Readings*,(by Hendrickson Publishers, 1995)

2. Sarah Young, *Jesus Calling: Enjoying The Peace Of His Presence*, (Nashville, TN: Thomas Nelson, Inc., 2004)

3. Charles R. Swindoll, *Bedside Blessings*, (Nashville, TN: Thomas Nelson, Inc., 2002)

4. Sarah Young, *Dear Jesus*, (Nashville, TN: Thomas Nelson, Inc., 2008)

5. John Eldredge, *The Ransomed Heart: A Collection of Devotional Readings*, (Nashville, TN: Thomas Nelson, Inc., 2005)

6. Jim Stephens, *GraceNotes: 365 Daily Devotionals*, (Maitland, FL, Xulon Press, 2011), Purchase at: www.resourceministries. org, or Amazon.com

7. Neil T. Anderson and Rich Miller, *Walking in Freedom, A 21 Day Devotional*, (Ventura, CA, Regal Books, 1999)

8. C. S. Lewis, *The Business of Heaven: Daily Readings from C. S. Lewis*, Edited by Walter Hooper, (London, Harcourt, Inc.)

9. C. S. Lewis, *George Macdonald: An Anthology, 365 Readings*, (New York, NY, HarperCollins Publishers, 1946)

10. John Eldredge, *Knowing The Heart Of God: A Year of Devotional Readings to Help You Abide In Him*, (Nashville, TN: Thomas Nelson, Inc., 2009)

11. God Maps, available free from www.jerichoventures.com

Spiritual Warfare

1. Chris Hayward, *God's Cleansing Stream: Developing a Life-Changing Deliverance Ministry in Your Church*, (Ventura, CA, Regal Books, 2003)

2. Neil T. Anderson, *Victory Over the Darkness: Realizing The Power of Your Identity in Christ*, (Ventura, CA, Regal Books, 1990)

3. Neil T. Anderson, *The Bondage Breaker: Overcoming Negative Thoughts, Irrational Feelings, Habitual Sins*, (Eugene, OR, Harvest House Publishers, 1990)

4. Chester and Betsy Kylstra, *Biblical Healing and Deliverance: A Guide To Experiencing Freedom*, (Grand Rapids, MI, Baker Publishing Group, 2005)

5. Francis Frangipane, *The Three Battlegrounds*, (Cedar Rapids, IA, Arrow Publications, Twenty Ninth Printing, July 2002)

6. Rebecca Brown, M.D. and Daniel Yoder, *Unbroken Curses: Hidden Source of Trouble in the Christian's Life*, (New Kensington, PA, Whitaker House, 1995)

7. Ron Phillips, *Vanquishing the Enemy: Triumphant in the Battles of Life*, (Cleveland, TN, Pathway Press, 1997)

8. Jim Logan, *Reclaiming Surrendered Ground*, (Chicago, IL, Moody Press, 1995)

9. Chuck D. Pierce and Rebecca Wagner Sytsema, *Ridding Your Home of Spiritual Darkness*, (Colorado Springs, CO, Wagner Publications,2000)

APPENDIX B Journal Examples

FYI: [I have used brackets '[ ]' to add additional comments or explanations to these examples of journaling.]

1/5. – Emotionally distant. [Earlier this year, I became aware of a tendency to maintain emotional distance from others. The following are some of the Journal entries that I've made regarding this issue.]

This is an insight while re-reading the Walking with God workbook, page 69. I tend to be attracted to people who are somewhat more emotionally distant or not as openly affectionate – like my parents. The original lies/agreements made about being less emotional/loving must have come from really early because of the words I have used to describe love/affection – "gooey, mushy": childish words. For years, Spock was my favorite character on Star Trek.

Q: Jesus what is this about? Please continue to speak truth to me about this.

1/7. Emotionally distant (continued)

Potential stronghold: "It is not good, okay to be affectionate, to be touchy-feely... I need to focus on being rational, emotionally distant – it is safer that way - then I won't be so easily hurt by others rejection or failing to return the affection I offer. There is punishment and pain associated with emotional attachment that is too close. It is not okay to give myself completely to anyone – maintain a safe distance – it is not safe to love anyone completely – even God." This is associated with my past stronghold of "all love is conditional" - part of the nest of lies. Part of this was dealt with, but, apparently, part remained to be dealt with till now. Jesus what else do you want me to see?

Thoughts: this is broader than simply not effusively showing affection it also involves not getting too close to others or letting them get too close to me – i.e. emotional distance. I have justified it by thinking it allows me to be more "objective". I recognized a few months ago that the attunement I have been able to show others (and myself) was shallow at best and usually less than fully real. I now know why. This might have started with severe spankings when I was a child and, since, have been reinforced throughout my life by my parents example and other experiences. Jesus please come into this place with me and show me the truth. Stay with me on this.

1/14. (Reference back to 1/7)

The (partial?) truth statement (so far) for the lie that "It is not good or okay to be affectionate loving or relate too intimately with others or even God: Intimacy/love with God and others is what we all need – is what I was created for. To reject that is to cooperate with Satan, hurt/reject God, and rob myself of love and all that comes with it." Lord, I sense that "intimacy/love" is to be my special focus for this year. I thank you Lord for this truth (Your personal rhema and logos). Thank you for this truth statement and for the tearing down of this latest stronghold Lord, I'm willing to look for the next one whenever you're ready.

Appendix B – Journal Examples (cont.)

1/22. – The next question.

As I continue to re-read Walking with God, I am reminded to ask the next question(page 203 top). Too often, I grab part of God's direction and charge off without getting the rest of his direction. Lord, please help me not to do that. With regard to intimacy affection, Lord, how do you want me to be more affectionate (with Pauline for example)? In what ways? When? Under what conditions? Lord, I recognize a self-centered selfish motive behind all this I repent of that. Help me to be more affectionate and develop deeper relationships simply because that is your will – not because there is some payoff/benefit for me.

1/25. "Over" and "now" [As in 'over-compensate', 'over-achieve', and I want what I want 'NOW'.]

God has brought these are two words me back to my attention for more work. There is more work to be done – more healing needed Q: Lord, what else do you want to do with these two words in my life? A: part of the answer is that "now" is a strength being over–used! Quick response/ goal orientation is part of my natural personality. This is also a spirit of control taking advantage of a natural part of my temperament. Q: Lord, what other strengths are being over–used? What habits do you want me to focus on breaking? What a joy and blessing it is to cooperate with God in this process!

2/1. Additional truth statement related to fear/avoidance of intimacy.

I'm seeing additional detail on this area that I need to look at: I long for love. And, at the same time I fear it – (motivation behind the prior stronghold): I held back from it; because accepting love brings "obligation" – responsibility. Then I have to "perform/measure up/earn love." Addition to prior Truth statement: With God, all I have to do is love him back. Move into him and let him (Holy Spirit) move into me. Then he provides both the will and the power to do whatever he wants done. No earning. No performance. No obligation. No responsibility. Just cooperation, willingness to allow, to connect, to hear, to act as he leads and provides whatever is needed. Freedom. Trust. Peace. Joy. Rest.

Refer to one 1/7. – The "maintaining of emotional distance" stronghold is (was ?) strongly really related to a need for deeper healing regarding the control stronghold that I thought had been fully dealt with. When the emotional distance stronghold was revealed and dealt with it allowed the control issue to surface for another look.

2/22. An additional truth statement to deal with the spirit of control:

Truth statement regarding control: Any control I think I have is an allusion! My next breath or heartbeat is not guaranteed. God's "control" is the only control that is safe and the only control that truly exists because only He is truly sovereign. Q: Jesus, you have given me a truth statement to deal with a stronghold that I haven't recognized yet. What are the stronghold(s) related to this truth statement that I need to see? Reference notes on P. 68 of the Desire Journal.

Appendix B – Journal Examples (cont.)

2/14. Overreactions (control related stronghold)

Candy [our rescue dog] is very resistant to being house trained. When she makes a mess, I feel angry and frustrated and I feel like punishing her more severely than I should. When others don't cooperate with my attempts to "help" them, I feel similar feelings of anger and frustration although I rarely show it. I almost never act on these feelings but they are there. Counseling examples include two people I can think of right now. It seems to be related to some sort of "control" issue that needs to surface so that it can be dealt with. Q: Jesus, what is this all about? What am I being triggered by? I feel pretty sure that it is really has little to do with counselees not cooperating. The clue that there is a stronghold there is my overreaction (at least at an emotional level). Also, because I am triggered by these behaviors, this comes from a memory with toxic content. I am not being completely genuine in my attunement to others. The attunement I do offer seems to have a controlling motive behind it. "Just cooperate with me so I can get you fixed up" (through a process). I use knowledge, good communication skills/practice to manipulate, intimidate, and "lead" others in the cooperating. Over reaction is a problem. But, it is not the root problem it is a symptom not a cause. It is a sad truth that, today, much of our medical practice and religious institutions are focused on treating symptoms rather than causes. Far too many of our churches tell us to repress desire, follow rules, live by duty and obligation, show the "right" external behaviors, etc., Instead of embracing desire and helping people discover their strongholds in deal with them. Father, Jesus, Holy Spirit please help me to discern what is going on with this.

3/6 – something hidden.

As I was reading and thinking about how the spirit of control affects those he has in bondage, it was noted that people try to exercise control because they feel naked/exposed. At first, I thought that this didn't apply to me and then I was reminded of recurring and vivid dreams I have had on and off earlier in my life of being naked (in groups of people) from the waist down – of how I would sneak around and try to find ways to cover my nakedness. At this point, all I have is questions and speculations about what this dream is about. Jesus please help me with this. What does it mean? What do you want to show me through it? I was reminded of this dream when I was asking about what stronghold (lies) were related to control that you wanted to reveal so they could be replaced with the truth you already provided. So, I think there must be a clue there. Reference 2/14 and other journaling related to control issues. Lord I want these control issues and related strongholds torn down! Lord, help me please. Also, are there toxic memories related to this?

3/9 – "independence"

In response to a question in the desire Journal, "what would make you feel really vulnerable and shaky to lose?" I listed several things. Then, I wrote "loss of independence" as a summary. Then an immediate rhema thought came: this is a clue to an unrecognized stronghold and is related to control issues and the related spirit of

Appendix B – Journal Examples (cont.)

control foothold". Jesus what is this all about? Please show me more about this. I want to be free from all strongholds and footholds related to control – as you reveal them and guide me through the process in Your own strategic time. At least part of the truth statement is that independence, like control, is a figment of my imagination and selfish nature. Even to seek it is a great failing. It is too easily overused and misused. It can lead to a functional independence from God. This "control" issue is related to the stronghold that I have dealt with in the past but still needs more work it's also related to a prior stronghold that "If God doesn't provide it for me that is up to me to provide for myself". Lord, what is it from that prior nest of lies that I still need to see?

3/ 23/13. Future focus.

It has occurred to me that my current assignment to help others find freedom from lies and demonic bondage is so very appropriate for the reading I'm now doing as part of the Journey of Desire Journal and Workbook. I have been considering what assignment I might be given in heaven where there will be no need to rid ourselves of lies and bondage. I realized how time–bound my current assignment is. So, my future focus will be something new. How exciting! I love to learn and apply truth in practical ways. I love music. I love solving problems. What sort of "problems" will there be in heaven? I love solving puzzles. Just think of the "puzzles" God could create for his puzzle-solvers. I think of the computer puzzle "*MYST*" and its subsequent series of puzzle-adventures. How I enjoyed visiting those beautiful digital "world's" to explore and solve their mysteries and problems. I only know that whatever God has for me to do, it will be perfectly suited for who God is made me to be. Whatever I do then will be exactly what he made me "for". And, it will bring honor and glory to Him; and it will be exquisitely joyful and fulfilling for me. Thank you Lord!!

[I hope reading the above sample of 'real-life' examples has been helpful. Keep your journaling simple and conversational. It illustrates how God usually reveals things to us over an extended period of time. My own journaling is more often just the recording of my thoughts and insights (sometimes just "musings') from something God has shown me that I don't want to forget or lose access to or that I think I might want to develop further later.]

APPENDIX C

Typical Strongholds and Footholds1

Instructions: Read down through this list and check off any that you think might apply to what you believe or how you feel. Then transfer each potential stronghold to your journal. Ask God the questions you have about each and about what the truth statements are that He wants to replace each with. You may also want to present your list to a Christian therapist, life coach, pastor, or other counselor who understands the things you are learning in this book.

Beliefs about Ourselves

Theme: Rejection, not belonging

- ☐ If I feel something like fear or hurt or frustration it's a sign of weakness. Failure is a sign of weakness. If I'm weak at all, I'll be rejected.

- ☐ I have a tendency to avoid close relationships because I might be rejected.

- ☐ One of my greatest fears is being abandoned.

- ☐ I avoid activities that require social interactions so I won't be rejected.

- ☐ I don't belong. I will always be on the outside (left out).

- ☐ I am/feel flawed; no one could possibly like me.

- ☐ Every failure verifies that I am flawed. If someone rejects me it also proves that I am flawed.

- ☐ I sometimes accept unpleasant tasks to please others and to avoid rejection.

- I am a bad person. If you knew the real me, you would reject me.

- I wear a 'mask' (to cover up), so people won't find out how horrible I am and reject me.

- People shouldn't wallow in their problems; they need to pull themselves up by their bootstraps (pretend they are something they are not) to be accepted.

- I can avoid conflict that would risk losing others' approval by being passive and not doing anything that might result in others rejecting me.

- I rarely express disagreement with others so I won't be rejected.

- The best way to avoid more hurt or rejection is to isolate myself.

- Any additional strongholds or footholds concerning this theme:

  _____

  _____

Theme: Unworthiness, guilt, shame, self-hatred, self-rejection

- No one will love me or care about me just for myself.

- I will always be lonely. The special man (woman) in my life will not be there for me.

- I am not worthy of love. I am not capable of getting the love I need without being either angry or clingy.

- I am unable to handle things on my own.

- I am/feel incompetent.

- If I feel embarrassed, it will be overwhelming and unbearable.

- I like the being center of attention. If I'm not, then I don't feel worthy or lovable.

- I am not worthy to receive anything from God.

- I am the problem. When something is wrong, it is my fault.

- God doesn't care about me. He's not involved in my life. He'll let me down, just like everyone else in this world.

- I have messed up so badly that I have missed God's best for me.

- The reason I'm being hurt is that there is something fundamentally wrong with me. I am really a bad person; nothing I do is right.

- I will always be (angry, shy, jealous, insecure, fearful, etc.).

- I am dirty, soiled, 'damaged goods'. I'm not worthy of love or acceptance.

- I feel _____ (guilt, shame, fearful, self-hatred, self-rejection, self-condemnation, bitterness, sorrow, depressed …) a lot of the time.

- Any additional strongholds or footholds concerning this theme:

  _____

  _____

Theme: Doing things (performing, achieving, …) to get self-worth, value, recognition

- I often feel the need to seek assurance, nurture, and support.

- I need to seek advice before making any decision.

- I will never get credit for what I do.

- I often envy others success.

- I agree with the saying that, "The one who dies with the most toys wins."

- Sometimes I daydream about fame, fortune, and power.

- I'm very sensitive to criticism and I can respond with intense anger (even if I don't show it).

- My value is in what I do. I am valuable only because I do things for others, or because I am "successful."

- Even when I do or give my best, it is often not good enough. I can never meet the standard.

- I have to always be fun and exciting if I want others to want to like me.

- God doesn't care if I have a "secret life" as long as I appear to be good.

- I can get the love and acceptance I want by over-achieving (or by _____).

- To feel good about myself, I must be successful at everything I do.

- I always let myself down; I'll never get back up.

- No matter how hard I try, nothing I do is right.

- I can never do anything right. Why should I ever try again?

- Nothing will ever work out the way I want it to.

- I've never done anything worthwhile. I'm a nobody.

- Any additional strongholds or footholds concerning this theme:

  _____

  _____

Theme: Control (to avoid hurt) or to get what I want

- I need to keep others at a distance emotionally.

- When I get in a conflict, it's 'my way or the highway'.

- The path to success involves lots of attention to details, order, and organization.

- I often procrastinate because I have such high standards for performance.

- I fear that I might not 'measure-up'.

- I don't delegate often because I can usually do things better than others.

- I am not capable of getting the love I need without being angry or clingy.

- This is a cold and dangerous world where people will hurt me and disaster will strike at any time, so I either need to play it safe and stay close to those who are stronger or wiser or isolate myself.

- ☐ I have to plan every day of my life. I have to continually plan or strategize. I can't relax.
- ☐ I don't disclose intimate thoughts or feelings because I might become vulnerable to being hurt all over again.
- ☐ Vulnerability opens me up to criticism and misinterpretation.
- ☐ The perfect life is one in which no conflict is allowed - so there is peace.
- ☐ I use _____ (food, drugs, sex ...) to make myself feel better.
- ☐ I use _____(anger, guilt, shame threats, fear, abuse, ...) to get what I want.
- ☐ Any additional strongholds or footholds concerning this theme:

_____

_____

Theme: Physical attractiveness

- ☐ I have to pay a lot of attention to my physical appearance because

_____

- ☐ I always want to stay looking young.
- ☐ I am unattractive. God shortchanged me.
- ☐ I am doomed to have certain physical disabilities. They are just part of what I have inherited.
- ☐ It is impossible for me to lose weight (or gain weight). I am just stuck.
- ☐ I am not competent or complete as a man (or woman) because _____

_____

- • Any additional strongholds or footholds concerning this theme:

_____

_____

Theme: Personality traits

- ☐ It's very difficult for me to really show empathy for other people.
- ☐ I really am uncomfortable with emotions.
- ☐ I have difficulty displaying affection toward others.
- ☐ The best defense is to attack first.
- ☐ Sometimes I am accused of being blunt or harsh.
- ☐ I struggle with impatience.
- ☐ I can be too excitable or emotional.
- ☐ I often talk too much.
- ☐ I have been accused of being manipulative.
- ☐ I tend to resist change.
- ☐ I have difficulty making decisions.
- ☐ I am too easily manipulated.
- ☐ I can be overly dependent.
- ☐ I tend to worry too much.
- ☐ I am easily hurt.
- ☐ I tend to fear criticism.
- ☐ I have been accused of being too critical.
- ☐ Any additional strongholds or footholds concerning this theme:

  _____

  _____

Theme: Identity

- ☐ I need lots of praise from other people to feel okay about myself.
- ☐ I should have been a boy (or girl). Then my parents would have valued me or loved me more.
- ☐ Men (women) have it better because _____
- ☐ I will never be known or appreciated for my real self

- ¤ I will never really change and be like God wants me to be because I will continue to struggle with _____ _____.

- ¤ I am strongly impacted by the opinions of others.

- ¤ I am helpless when I'm alone.

- ¤ Any additional strongholds or footholds concerning this theme:

  _____

  _____

Theme: Miscellaneous

- ¤ I pretty much see things as all-or-nothing - either or black-or-white.

- ¤ I'm turned off or are fearful by tenderness or touch.

- ¤ I need a strong protector to care and do things for me.

- ¤ I have wasted a lot of time and energy, some of my best years.

- ¤ Turmoil is normal for me.

- ¤ I don't need others I can make it on my own

- ¤ Some people think I have an inflated sense of self-worth.

- ¤ I will always have financial problems.

- ¤ I will always have health problems.

- ¤ I will die younger than I should.

- ¤ I have been or am now involved with _____ (witchcraft, fortune telling, Satan worship ...).

- ¤ I will go to heaven because _____ _____ (I follow all my church's rules, I have done more good things than bad, I belong to and attend a church, I'm a 'good' person ...).

- ¤ Any additional strongholds or footholds concerning this theme.

  _____

  _____

Beliefs about Others:

- ¤   Theme: Safety/Protection
- ¤   I must be very guarded about what I say, because anything I say may be used against me by others.
- ¤   I must guard and hide my emotions and feelings from others.
- ¤   I don't want to give anyone the satisfaction of knowing that they have wounded or hurt me. I'll not be vulnerable, humiliated or shamed.
- ¤   I don't need others to be happy. Others may hurt me.
- ¤   Any additional strongholds or footholds concerning this theme:

  _____

  _____

Theme: Retaliation

- ¤   The correct way to respond if someone offends me is to punish them by getting mad, by withdrawing from them, cutting them off, getting even in any way I can.
- ¤   I will make sure that (insert a person's name) hurts as much as I do!
- ¤   I don't get mad - I just get even.
- ¤   When others don't meet my needs or hurt me, I feel _____ _____ (angry, bitter, unforgiving, condemning …).
- ¤   Any additional Strongholds or footholds concerning this theme:

  _____

  _____

Theme: Victim

- ¤   Stuff just happens to me and I can do little, if anything, to change it.
- ¤   My feelings don't count. No one cares what I feel.
- ¤   Others will humiliate me and violate me.

- Others will just use, control, and abuse me.

- My value is based totally on others' judgment/perception of me.

- I am completely under other people's authority/control. I have no will or choice of my own.

- If something goes wrong or others hurt me, I just have to suck it up and move on – no whining.

- I will not be known, understood, loved or appreciated for who I am by those close to me.

- Others always think about themselves first. They always treat me like my feelings don't count.

- I know others don't usually like me. There's no use trying.

- The past will always repeat itself.

- I can't count on others. They believe I'm fundamentally flawed. They will always let me down.

- I'm not going to reach out to others any more they'll just slap me down again.

- No matter what I do to please others, it doesn't make any difference. I'm always walking on egg shells. It is best just not care.

- Any additional strongholds or footholds concerning this theme:

  _____

  _____

Theme: Hopelessness/helplessness

- Others will always be unable or unwilling to meet my needs.

- Others are not trustworthy or reliable.

- Others are abusive, and I deserve it.

- Others will always let you down, just when you need them most.

- Others are not trustworthy; they are unreliable when it comes to meeting my needs.

- Others are either unwilling or incapable of loving me.

- I am out here all alone. If I get into trouble or need help, there is no one to rescue me.

- I can't rely on others I have to make it on my own.

- Others are capable of meeting my needs but might not do so because of my flaws.

- Others are trustworthy and reliable but might abandon me because of my worthlessness.

- Any additional strongholds or footholds concerning this theme:

  _____

  _____

Theme: Defectiveness in relationships

- One or both of my parents ever hugged me or told me they loved me.

- I will never be able to fully give or receive love.

- I don't know what love is.

- If I let anyone get close to me, I may get my heart broken again. I can't let myself risk it.

- If I fail to please you, I won't receive your pleasure and acceptance of me. Therefore, I have to be perfect. I have to do whatever is necessary to try to please others.

- Any additional strongholds or footholds concerning this theme:

  _____

  _____

Theme: God

- God loves other people more than He loves me.

- God only values me for what I do. My life is just a means to an end.

- No matter how much I try, I'll never be able to do enough or perform well enough to please God.

- God is judging me when I relax. I have to stay busy about His work or He will punish me.

- God has let me down before. He may do it again. I can't trust Him or feel secure with Him.

- Any additional strongholds or footholds concerning this theme:

  _____

  _____

APPENDIX D

Small Group Discussion Questions

Note to discussion group leader: If possible, each group member should have a journal to record important insights gained as these questions are discussed. If needed, time should be given during the discussion sessions to reflect on these insights and record them. Don't get in too big a hurry. Allow any group member to request time to briefly journal their thoughts. Depending on the number of people in the group and how open they are to sharing their feelings and experience, any given chapter's discussion may take several sessions to complete.

Introduction:

Someone read aloud the 'Story' on pages 1 and 2.

1. When did you personally become really aware of the spiritual realm?

2. Did it make any difference in the way you lived?

3. When did you first become aware that sometimes your thoughts were not from your own mind? To what source did you attribute them?

4. Is freedom will *really* necessary for there to be true love? Why or why not?

5. When you first heard about Jesus dying in your place, what did you think? How did the idea of a 'substitutionary' death strike you? This is usually a difficult concept in 'Western' culture.

Read the C. S. Lewis' quote on page 2.

6. What did you think about C.S. Lewis' statement that we are potentially creatures that we might be tempted to worship? What else struck you about it?

Read the paragraph at the bottom of page 2.

7. Have you ever consciously made a commitment to live your life based on reality and truth? If you did, would you be willing to tell us about the circumstances in your life that led you to that commitment?

8. What other comments or thoughts do you have about the introduction?

Small Group Discussion Questions (cont.)
Chapter 1 - Reality

As you read this chapter,

1. What did you feel?

2. What did you learn?

3. What did you want?

4. What did you understand that you hadn't understood before? What questions were raised in your mind that you would like to know more about?

5. Did you ever think that Christianity was just a myth? If so, what changed your mind?

6. After reading this chapter, what questions do you have about the 'big picture' of reality?

Chapter 2 – Mind Attack

1. When we choose to join God's side, Satan's attacks are focused on us in ways that they were not before. What have these attacks been in your life?

2. What changes did you see in your life when you received Jesus as your personal savior and lord – when you had your human spirit restored and you received the Holy Spirit?

3. Some people see immediate, mayor changes in their lives. Others, not so much. Either way we enter into a process that the Bible calls 'sanctification'. What is the purpose of sanctification? What does God use to sanctify us? How long does it take to become 'sanctified'?

Small Group Discussion Questions (cont.)

4. What strategy did Satan use on Adam and Eve? What is the primary strategy he has used on mankind ever since then? Why is he still using it today?

5. What did you learn about processing painful experiences?

6. What process goes on in our brain-mind-spirit that sets us up to believe things that are not true? The worst thing about these false explanations is that they are hiding in our implicit, 'invisible' memories – in our blind spots; and affecting our behavior without us even being aware of it. How did it make you feel to recognize this truth?

7. Where does 'temptation' come from?

8. What are 'strongholds'?

9. What are the consequences of sin?

10. What is a 'foothold'?

Chapter 3 – Resources

1. What is the purpose of our spiritual resources?

2. When we use spiritual resources to defeat demonic influence, whose power are we using? What is the danger if we begin to think it is *our* power?

3. Whose 'authority' have we been given? Who gave it to us?

4. What 'power' to we have resident within each of us?

5. What 'position' do we have in Jesus?

6. Given our authority, power and position as Christians acting in Jesus' name, what are the chances that a demon doesn't have to obey us when speak in Jesus' name?

Small Group Discussion Questions (cont.)

7. Review and discuss each piece of spiritual armor we are to put on. Pantomime putting on your armor.

8. Can some of the promises given in the Old Testament apply to Christians today? How? Explain your answer.

9. What is the difference between the Greek words '*logos*' and '*rhema*'?

10. Does God actually 'speak' to Christians today (in the 21st century)? How does He do this?

11. What is the one thing you always have to do with any "word" that you think you have heard from God?

12. What is the 'fruit' of the Spirit? What is the first 'fruit' mentioned in Col. 5:21? Describe this kind of "love". Is it an emotion or a set of behaviors? (Ref. 1Cor. 13)

13. Why is 'unforgiveness' such a problem?

14. What is 'generational sin'? Why is it a problem?

Chapter 4 – Footholds

1. Just as a review, what is a foothold?

2. How can we get rid of a foothold?

3. What are each of the four 'Rs' used in the process of getting rid of a foothold? What does each 'R' accomplish?

4. What is a 'soul tie'? How can we get rid of soul ties?

Chapter 5 – Strongholds

1. Just as a review, what is a stronghold?

Small Group Discussion Questions (cont.)

2. How do we establish a stronghold?

3. What is a 'word curse'? Why are word curses dangerous?

4. How does asking ourselves questions help us discover strongholds?

5. Why should we go to all the work of journaling as we go through this process?

6. What 'substitutes' are you aware of in your life? Does someone have the courage to share examples of their substitutes with the group?

7. What are your assumptions about what God's job is in your life? What are the dangers associated with the wrong assumptions?

8. Ask yourself, "What are the things in my life, or in my desires, or in my dreams that I think would make me happy without God?" What things did you feel that way about in the past?

9. Ask yourself, "What thought or idea have I agreed with that would allow me to have the things or relationships I want *now* apart from God?" If possible, journal about these things so you don't lose touch with them. If not, do it as soon as you can. These are the very things that can become our addictions, our substitutes, our idols if we allow them to.

10. What do I privately fear that God might take away? What does God want to say to you about your answers to this question? If you don't know, ask Him.

11. What can we learn from our dreams, daydreams, or fantasies?

12. What can we learn from the things that go wrong in our lives?

13. What are you allowing to side-track you from single-mindedly pursuing this process of getting free?

Small Group Discussion Questions (cont.)

14. Have you recognized a stronghold in your own life yet? Would you be willing to share it with the group along with the truth statement related to it? This can be an embarrassing and

intimidating thing to do – so, only do it if you feel God is asking you to do it. Your openness can be more helpful and freeing to others than you can possibly imagine.

15. Why is it so hard to be a 'good' Christian while, at the same time, insisting on your right to control your own life? What is wrong with the statement, "It is God's job to *help me* live a good Christian life?

16. What is wrong with the statement, "What really matters is that my behavior is what it should be – that it conforms to what would be Christ-like - loving God – loving people"?

17. Would someone be willing to share with the group a time when they know they were under a spiritual attack? How did you deal with it?

18. How should we deal with normal personality characteristics or other areas of natural strengths that we are over-using or misusing?

19. What is the 'formula' for getting rid of a stronghold?

20. Have you ever actually, specifically forgiven your ancestors for all the 'garbage' (sinful influences) they have passed down to you? If not, go to step three of the process for getting rid of a stronghold and pray a prayer like the one included there.

21. What is 'taking thoughts captive' (2 Cor. 10:5) all about?

Small Group Discussion Questions (cont.)

22. Why do we speak out loud and keep our eyes open when we are doing spiritual warfare?

Chapter 6 – Memories

1. What kind of memories needs healing?

2. What does 'time travel' have to do with the healing of memories?

3. Why is it safe to go back in time and re-experience horrible memories with Jesus?

4. How do we benefit by re-visiting a toxic memory with Jesus?

5. Is a sinful habit something we can simply tell to leave, like a lie (stronghold) we can replace with truth, or a bondage to demonic influence (foothold) we can simply break using God's authority and power? What does breaking a sinful habit involve?

Chapter 7 – Staying Free

1. What was the bad news? What was the Good news?

2. What is God's purpose for the bad stuff?

3. What sort of change happens in our brain when we focus on a God of love?

4. What was your 'gut-level' response to the idea that God keeps working in our lives at deeper and deeper levels?

5. The process of getting free places a lot of focus on us personally. What is an important secondary purpose of us getting free?

6. What part does continually exposing ourselves to God's truth have in our being able to stay free?

Small Group Discussion Questions (cont.)

7. Why bother to journal?

8. How many ways can you think of to get rid of sinful habits?

9. Romans 12:1-2 talks about us being 'transformed' by the renewing of our mind. Recent discoveries is medical science has revealed that our brains are literally changed by the things we choose to think about. How does this work?

10. When you recognize a thought that you don't want in your mind, what can you do about it?

11. What is one of our greatest dangers as we begin to be successful in getting rid of foothold, strongholds, and toxic memories? What can we do about it when we realize that we have been tripped-up by that danger?

End Notes:

Introduction

1. John 3:27 NKJV
2. 1 Cor. 4:7 NIV
3. 1 Cor. 13:12 NLT
4. Matt 13:11-12 NIV

Chapter 1 - Reality

1. 2 Tim. 3:16 NIV
2. From the essay "Myth Become Fact" C. S. Lewis, God in the Dock: Essays on Theology and Ethics (Grand Rapids, MI: Erdmann, 1970), 66-67.
3. John Eldredge, *Epic, The Story God Is Telling*, (Nashville, TN: Thomas Nelson, Inc., 2004), 99-100
4. C. S. Lewis, *Meer Christianity*, (New York, NY: Simon & Schuster, Inc., 1980), 63
5. Kenneth Richard Samples, *A World of Difference , Putting Christian Truth-claims to the Worldview Test*, (Grand Rapids, MI, Baker Publishing Group, 2007)
6. Gen. 1:1-2 NIV
7. Heb. 11:3 NIV
8. Gen. 1: 26-27 NIV; For an excellent discussion of what being made in the Image of God implies, see Kenneth Richard Samples, *7 Truths That Changed The World*, (Grand Rapids, MI, Baker Publishing Group, 2012), Chapter 11.
9. John 1:1-3 NIV
10. John 1:14, Col. 1:16 NIV
11. Ezek. 38:15 NIV
12. Rev. 12:9 NIV
13. Exod. 3:13-14 NIV

14. Deut. 33:27, Psa. 90:2 NIV

15. 1Kings 8:27, Jer. 23:24 NIV

16. Ps. 50:10-12 NIV

17. Ps. 139:7-12 NIV

18. Rev. 19:6 NIV

19. Ps. 139:2-6, Isa. 46:9-10 NIV

20. Prov. 2:6, Rom. 16:27 NIV

21. Heb. 1:10-12, Heb. 13:8 NIV

22. Isa. 46:9-10 NIV

23. Lev. 19:2, 1Peter 1:15-16 NIV

24. John 14:6, John 17:3 Titus 1:1-2 NIV

25. Deut. 7:9, Psa. 89:1-2 NIV

26. John 3:16, Rom. 5:8, 1John 3:1, 1 Cor. Chapter 13 defines this special kind of Godly Love.

27. Ps. 111:4 NIV

28. Ps. 103:8-17 NIV

29. Ps. 119:137, Rom. 11:22 NIV

30. 2 Cor. 13:14, Matt. 28:19, NIV

31. Neh. 9:6 NIV

32. Mark. 13:32 NIV

33. 1 Pet. 1:4 NIV

34. Morris, L. L. (1996). *Heaven*. In D. R. W. Wood, I. H. Marshall, A. R. Millard, J. I. Packer & D. J. Wiseman (Eds.), New Bible dictionary (D. R. W. Wood, I. H. Marshall, A. R. Millard, J. I. Packer & D. J. Wiseman, Ed.) (3rd ed.) (457). Leicester, England; Downers Grove, IL: Intervarsity Press.

35. Gen. 1:28 NIV

36. Gen. 2:16 & 17 NIV

37. Gen. Chapter 3 NIV

38. 1 John 5:19 NIV

39. Ps. 8:4-8 NIV

40. Eph. 1:4-5, Rom. 8:29 NIV

41. Samples, *7 Truths That Changed The World*, 168

42. Ibid, 171-2; Rom. 8:8 NIV

43. C. S. Lewis, *The Joyful Christian*, (New York, NY, Macmillan Publishing Company, Inc., 1977), 215+

44. Rom. 6:16 – 23; 1John 5:19 NIV

45. Lewis, *Meer Christianity*, 53

46. Samples, *7 Truths That Changed The World*, 172

47. Rom. 3:23 NIV

48. Rom. 6:23 NIV

49. John 3: 16-18 NIV

50. 1 Pet. 3:18 MSG

51. John 1:12 NIV

52. Matt. 5:48 NIV

53. Lewis, *Mere Christianity*, 176

54. John 10:10 NIV

55. John Eldredge, *The Sacred Romance*, (Nashville, TN: Thomas Nelson, Inc., 2004) 119 - 120

56. Heb. 2:14-15, NIV

57. Rev. 21,NIV

58. 1 John 4:4; Luke 10:19 NIV

59. Ezekiel 28:12-17; Isaiah 14:12-18; Rev. 12:7-9; Matt. 25:41; and Rev. 20:10 NIV

60. John Eldredge, *Waking The Dead*, (Nashville, TN: Thomas Nelson, Inc., 2003) 17

61. Ibid, 18

62. Eldredge, *The Sacred Romance*, 104-5

63. Eph. 6:10-12 NIV

64. Michael is the archangel who fought Satan in Heaven. Reference Rev. 12:7 NIV

65. Charles Haddon Spurgeon, *Morning and Evening: Daily Readings*,(by Hendrickson Publishers, 1995), 671

66. 1John 5:19-20; John 14:30 NIV

67. Luke 10:19 NIV

68. Rev. 20:10 NIV

69. Eldredge, *The Sacred Romance,* 108

70. John 18:36 NIV

71. John 3:16-20 NIV

72. Ray C. Stedman, *Talking with My Father*, (Grand Rapids, MI, Discovery House Publishers, 1997), 136.

Chapter 2 – Mind Attack

1. Sarah Young, *Jesus Calling: Enjoying The Peace Of His Presence*, (Nashville, TN: Thomas Nelson, Inc., 2004) 274

2. Francis Frangipane, *The Three Battlegrounds*, (Cedar Rapids, IA, Arrow Publications, Twenty Ninth Printing, July 2002) 3

3. Our original knowledge of God, righteousness, and holiness.

4. 2 Cor. 1:22; 1 Cor. 6:19 NIV

5. John 10:28-30

6. 2 Cor. 5:17 NIV

7. Rom. 8:29-30

8. Charles R. Swindoll, *Bedside Blessings*, (Nashville, TN: Thomas Nelson, Inc., 2002), 305

9. Eph. 6:12 NIV

10. John 14:6 NIV

11. John 8:31-2 NIV

12. Swindoll, *Bedside Blessings*, 306

13. Karl Lehman, M.D., *Outsmarting Yourself: Catching Your Past Invading The Present And What to Do About It*,(Libertyville, IL, This JOY! Books, 2011), 5-6

14. Ibid, 6 - 13

15. C. S. Lewis, *Meer Christianity*, (New York, NY: Simon & Schuster, Inc., 1980), 93

16. Lehman, *Outsmarting Yourself*, 15 - 16

17. ibid, 18

18. ibid,.21

19. ibid, 21

20. ibid, 22 - 25

21. ibid, 48

22. Lewis, *Meer Christianity*, 95

23. Eph. 2:1-3 NIV

24. 2 Cor. 4:4 NKJV

25. Eldredge, *The Sacred Romance*, 101

26. 2 Cor. 2:11 NIV

27. John Eldredge, Wild at Heart, (Nashville, TN: Thomas Nelson, Inc., 2001), 163

28. 2 Cor. 10:3–5 NIV

29. Friberg, Timothy ; Friberg, Barbara ; Miller, Neva F.: Analytical Lexicon of the Greek New Testament. Grand Rapids, Mich. : Baker Books, 2000 (Baker's Greek New Testament Library 4), S. 290

30. Isa. 59:2 NIV

31. Isa. 59:2 NIV

32. Isa. 59:2 NIV

33. Rom. 3:23 NIV

34. Rom. 8:8 NIV

35. John 8:34 NIV

36. Rom. 7:23 NIV

37. Eph. 4:26-27 NIV

38. Strong, J., *Enhanced Strong's Lexicon*, (Bellingham, WA: Logos Bible Software, 2001).

39. John 14:2 NLT

40. 1John 4:4 NIV

41. Rom. 7:15-19 & 21-25 NIV

42. Rom. 8:1-4 NIV

43. Their website is: www.cleansingstream.org

44. John 10:10 MSG

45. 1 Cor. 13:1-3 NIV

Chapter 3 - Resources

1. 2 Tim. 3:16-17 NIV

2. Lehman, *Outsmarting Yourself*, .252

3. 2 Pet. 1:3, NIV

4. John 15:5 NIV

5. 2 Cor. 12:9 AMP

6. James 4:7 NIV

7. 2 Cor. 4:7

8. Eph. 6:10-11 AMP

9. 1 Tim. 4:4-5 NIV

10. Luke 10:19 NIV

11. Wood, D. R. W., & Marshall, A. R. Millard, J. I. Packer & D. J. Wiseman (Eds.) *New Bible dictionary*, 3rd ed., (Downers Grove, IL: InterVarsity Press. 1996), 105–106

12. Mt. 28:18; Col. 2:10 NIV

13. Frangipane, *The Three Battlegrounds*, 2

14. Eph. 1:19 NIV

15. Wood, D. R. W., & Marshall, I. H. (1996). New Bible dictionary (3rd ed.) (945). Leicester, England; Downers Grove, IL: InterVarsity Press.

16. Eph. 1:19-23 NIV

17. Eph. 2:6 NIV

18. Eph. 1:21 NIV

19. Eph. 6:11 NIV

20. O'Brien, P. T., *The letter to the Ephesians. The Pillar New Testament Commentary* (Grand Rapids, MI: W.B. Eerdmans Publishing Co.,), 456–495

21. John Eldredge, *Walking With God*, (Nashville, TN: Thomas Nelson, Inc., 2008), 54

22. Eph. 6:10-18 NIV

23. Heb. 13:5 NIV

24. Eph. 2:14-18; 4:3-6 NIV

25. Heb 11:1 AMP

26. Eph. 2:8-10 NIV

27. Heb. 4:12 NIV

28. *The NASB Topical Index*, Electronic Edition, (La Habra, CA: The Lockman Foundation, 1998)

29. *Spiritual Gifts.*, In C. Draper, A. England, S. Bond, E. R. Clendenen & T. C. Butler (Eds.); *Holman Illustrated Bible Dictionary,* C. Draper, A. England, S. Bond, E. R. Clendenen & T. C. Butler, (Eds.), (Nashville, TN: Holman Bible Publishers, 2003), 1529

30. Heb 6:13-18 NIV

31. Rom. 4:16; Gal. 3:5-9 NIV

32. *Promise.* In D. R. W. Wood, I. H. Marshall, A. R. Millard, J. I. Packer & D. J. Wiseman (Eds.), Douglas, J. D., ed. *The New Bible Dictionary,* 2nd ed., (Downers Grove, IL: InterVarsity Press, 1996)

33. Rom. 4:9-25; Gal. 3:6-29 NIV

34. Rom. 4:16 NIV

35. Rom. 15:8-12 NIV

36. Rom. 9:4 NIV

37. Rom. 11:25-26 NIV

38. 2 Cor. 7:1 NIV

39. 39. Achtemeier, P. J., *Harper's Bible dictionary*, 1st ed., Harper & Row, & Society of Biblical Literature, (San Francisco: Harper & Row,1985) 825–826

40. 40.Vine, W., & Bruce, F., *Vine's Expository Dictionary of Old and New Testament Words*, Vol. 2, (Old Tappan NJ:, Revell, 1981), 230

41. 41.Rom. 8:28 NIV

42. 42. Eph. 2:8-9 NIV

43. Eph. 2:10 NIV

44. 1 Cor. 13:13 NIV

45. Heb. 1:1 NIV

46. Eph, 1:17 NIV

47. Prov., chapters 1 – 4. NIV

48. Eldredge, *Walking with God*, 204 - 205

49. Ibid, 13-14

50. Lehman, *Outsmarting Yourself*, 157 and 270+

51. Ibid, 157

52. Luke 12:29, NLT)

53. Eldredge, *Walking with God*, 201-203

54. Gal. 5:22-23 NIV

55. 1 Cor. 13:4-7 NIV

56. Gal. 5:6. NIV

57. Jerry Cook, *The Holy Spirit: So…What's The Big Deal*, (North Charleston, SC, CreateSpace Independent Publishing Platform, 2013)

58. Matt. 6:14-15 NIV

59. 1 John 1:9; 2 Cor. 7:1; Heb. 12:1-2 NIV

60. 1 John 2:2 NIV

61. Isa. 59:2 NIV

62. Isa. 59:2 NIV

63. Isa. 59:2 NIV

64. Rom. 3:23 NIV

65. Rom. 8:8 NIV

66. John 8:34, & 6:23; and Eph. 4:26 NIV

67. Bold Love, P.88

68. Ken Ellis, Avoiding The Dangers of Superficial Forgiveness, RBC Discovery Series, Copyright, 2004, RBC Ministries, Grand Rapids, Michigan.

69. Dr. Dan B. Allender and Dr. Tremper Longman III, *Bold Love*, (Colorado Springs, CO, NavPress,1992)

70. Exod. 20: 5b-6 NIV

71. Ezek. 18:20a NIV

72. Ryken, P. G., *Written in stone: The Ten commandments and today's moral crisis,* (Wheaton, IL, Crossway Books, 2003), 75–77

73. Rom. 13:1 & 5; Heb. 13:17; and 1 Pet. 2:13 NIV

74. Matt. 18:18 NIV

75. Eph. 4:26-27 NIV

76. Heb. 12:1, NIV

77. Matt. 18:19 NIV

Chapter 4 – Footholds

1. John 8:34 NIV

2. www.cleansingstream.org

3. Heb. 11:25 NIV

4. Rom. 8:29 NIV

5. Gen. 2:24 NIV

6. 1 John 1:9, NIV

7. James 4:7 NIV

Chapter 5 – Strongholds

1. Frangipane, *The Three Battlegrounds*, 9

2. Charles Stanley

3. Frangipane, *The Three Battlegrounds*, 29

4. John 8:44 NIV

5. *Cleansing Stream Seminar Workbook*, (Van Nuys, CA, Cleansing Stream Ministries, 2003) 3-17

6. Eldredge, *Walking With God*, 39

7. John Eldredge, *Beautiful Outlaw*, (New York, N.Y., FaithWords Hachette Book Group, 2011), 214

8. Luke 6:45 NIV

9. Matt. 15:19–20 MSG

10. Matt. 12:36 NIV

11. Rom. 10: 9-10 NIV

12. Prov. 18:21 NIV

13. James 3:5-11 NIV

14. *Cleansing Stream Seminar Workbook*, 3-30

15. Rom. 10:10 NIV

16. www.logos.com

17. 2 Cor. 10:5 MSG

18. Rom. 14:23b

19. Ephesians 5:26 NIV (my paraphrase)

20. John Eldredge, *The Journey of Desire: Searching For The Life We've Only Dreamed Of*, (Nashville, TN: Thomas Nelson, Inc., 2002), 30

21. C. S. Lewis, Paul F. Ford, Ed., *Yours, Jack – Spiritual Direction from C. S. Lewis*, (New York, NY, Harper Collins Publishers,2008), 355

22. John Eldredge, *Journey of Desire Journal and Guidebook*, (Nashville, TN: Thomas Nelson, Inc., 2002), 240

23. Gerald G. May, *The Wisdom of Wilderness: Experiencing The Healing Power Of Nature*, (New York, NY, Harper Collins Publishers,2006), 100

24. John 8:34; Eph. 4:26 NIV

25. Young, *Jesus calling*, 369

26. Matt. 7: 15-20 NIV

27. Gal. 5:21 NIV

28. Gal. 5:19-21 NIV

29. Rom. 7:20-23 MSG

30. Gal. 5:17 NIV

31. Eldredge, *The Journey of Desire*, 72

32. C. S. Lewis, *The Weight of Glory*, (New York, NY, Harper Collins Publishers,1976) 26, 29, 30, and 31

33. Dr. Dan B. Allender and Dr. Tremper Longman III, *Bold Love*, 169

34. ibid, 169

35. Eldredge, *Journey of Desire*, 171

36. Eldredge, *The Journey of Desire Journal and Workbook*, 43

37. Eldredge, *The Journey of Desire*, 35

38. Eldredge, *Walking With God*, 6, 7, and 86

39. ibid, 87

40. 1 Cor. 11:31–32 NIV

41. Matt. 2:12 NIV

42. Matt. 2:13 NIV

43. 2 Cor. 10:5 NIV

44. 1 Tim. 2:4, NLB

45. Eldredge, *The Sacred Romance*, 1

46. M. Scott Peck, *The Road Less Traveled*, (New York, NY, Harper Collins Publishers,1978), 249-251

47. John Eldredge, Utter *Relief of Holiness: How God's Goodness Frees Us from Everything that Plagues Us*,(New York, NY, FaithWorks Hachette Book Group, 2013), 54–55

48. Rom. 14:14 NIV

49. John 8:34; Eph. 4:26 NIV

50. Eldredge, *Walking With God*, 158

51. See Eldredge, *The Sacred Romance*, page 115 for an example of this.

52. Eldredge, *Beautiful Outlaw*, 160

53. Lewis, *The Weight of Glory*, 60- 61

54. 1 Cor. 14:29 NIV

55. 1Cor. 12:10, NIV

56. John 14:26, NIV

57. John Eldredge, *Walking with God Workbook*, (Nashville, TN: Thomas Nelson, Inc., 2008), 164

58. Rom. 14:23 NIV

59. Chester and Betsy Kylstra, *Biblical Healing and Deliverance: A Guide To Experiencing Freedom*, (Grand Rapids, MI, Baker Publishing Group, 2005), 126-129

60. Lewis, *Weight of Glory*, 162

61. Dr. Dan B. Allender and Dr. Tremper Longman III, *Bold Love*, 70-71

62. Luke 9:23-25 NIV

63. Lewis, *Meer Christianity*, 160-171.

64. Phil. 2:13 NIV

65. John 15:1-5; Phil 1:11 NIV

66. Matt. 15:18-20 NIV

67. 1 Chron. 28:9 NIV

68. 1 Cor. 13:4-8 NIV

69. Isa. 54:6 NIV

70. Rom. 8:1-2 NIV

71. 1 John 1:9 NIV

72. 2 Cor. 11:14-15 NIV

73. Eldredge, *The Utter Relief of Holiness*, 134-135

74. Eldredge, *Walking With God Workbook*, 115

75. Frangipane, *The Three Battlegrounds*, 31

76. Eph 1: 3-4 MSG; 1 Thess. 5:23 NIV

77. Eldredge, *Walking with God*, 34-36.

78. *Cleansing Stream Seminar Workbook*, 3-17 and 3-18

79. Eldredge, *The Utter Relief of Holiness*, 150

80. Rom. 8:29, Eph. 4:22-24 NIV; 1 John 3:2 NKJV

81. Luke 11:21-22 NIV

82. Frangipane, *The Three Battlegrounds*, 31

83. Lehman, *Outsmarting Yourself*, 323.

84. 2 Cor. 10:3-5 NIV

85. Brennan Manning, *Ruthless Trust: The Ragamuffin's Path to God*, (New York, NY, Harper Collins Publishers,2000), 171

86. Mart Dehaan, , *The Forgiveness of God*, (Grand Rapids, MI, Discovery Series, RBC Ministries,2007), 31

87. 2 Cor. 10:3-5 NIV

88. Rom. 8:27 NIV

Chapter 6 – Memories

1. 2 Cor. 3:17–18 NIV

2. Chester and Betsy Kylstra, *Restoring the Foundations: An Integrated Approach To Healing Ministry*, 2nd Edition, (Hendersonville, NC, Restoring The Foundations Publications, 2001), 230

3. Rom. 8:28 NIV

4. Gen. Chapters 37 to 50.

5. Gen. 50:19 NIV

6. Eldredge, *Walking With God*, 160

7. 1 John 1:3-7;Rom. 8:29 NIV

8. 1 Cor. 2:16; Phil. 2:5-8 NIV

9. Kylstra, *Restoring the Foundations*, 219

10. Lehman, *Outsmarting Ourselves*, 5- 6

11. Eldredge, *The Utter Relief of Holiness*, 147-8.

12. Eldredge, *Walking With God Workbook*, 132

13. ibid, 132-133

14. Deut. 4:29, Jer. 29:13, Matt. 7:7 NIV

15. John 8:32 NIV

16. Lehman, *Outsmarting Yourself*, 157

17. Eldredge, *The Sacred Romance Workbook and Journal*, 46

Chapter 7 – Staying Free

1. Christy Bower, *Best Friends with God: Falling in Love With the God Who Loves You*, (Grand Rapids, MI, Discovery House Publishers,2010), 104

2. Psa. 51:6 NIV

3. John 8:32 NIV

4. 2 Cor. 3:17-18 NIV

5. Rom. 8:28 NIV

6. 1 Pet. 4:12-13 NIV

7. John 16:33 NIV

8. Rom. 8:17-18 NIV

9. Phil 2:15 NIV

10. James 1:2-4 NIV

11. Dallas Willard, *The Devine Conspiracy: Discovering Our Hidden Life In God*, (New York, NY, HarperCollins Publishers, 1997), 386

12. Eldredge, *The Sacred Romance*, 152

13. Eldredge, *Walking With God*, 69

14. Jean-Pierre De Caussade, translated by Kitty Muggeridge, *The Sacrament of the Present Moment*, (San Francisco, California, Harper & Row, Publishers,1989), 56

15. Ibid, 84

16. Dr. Tim Clinton and Dr. Joshua Straub, *God Attachment: Why You Believe, Act, and Feel The Way You Do About God*, (New York, NY, Howard Books, 2010), 168

17. Timothy R. Jennings, M.D., *The God-Shaped Brain: How Changing Your View Of God Transforms Your Life*, (Downers Grove, IL, InterVarsity Press, 2013), 12

18. ibid, 27, 29

19. ibid, 58

20. 1 Pet. 4:12-13, MSG

21. Dr. Dan B. Allender and Dr. Tremper Longman III, *Bold Love*, 290

22. Rom. 8:37, NIV

23. Rev. 1:6 and 5:10 , *YLT*

24. Eph. 4:12-16, NIV

25. Eldredge, *The Sacred Romance*, 158.

26. Rick Joyner, *The Call*, (Charlotte, NC, Morning Star Publications, 1999), 138 & 142

27. Matt. 7:1-6; Luke 6:37-42 NIV

28. Rom 8:29 NIV

29. Heb. 12:29 NIV

30. George Macdonald, *Unspoken Sermons series*, Series I, II, III In One Volume, (Memphis, TN, Botton of the Hill Publishing, 2012), 15

31. Eldredge, *The Sacred Romance*, p. 203

32. ibid, 205

33. Lewis, *The Weight of Glory*, 91-115

34. James 4:7 NIV

35. Phil. 4:6-9 NIV

36. Jennings, *The God-Shaped Brain*, 65

37. 2 Cor. 10:5 NIV

38. Jennings, *The God-Shaped Brain*, p. 65

39. Jack W. Hayford, *The Hayford Bible Handbook*, (Nashville, TN: Thomas Nelson, Inc., 1995), 687

40. Sarah Young, *Dear Jesus*, (Nashville, TN: Thomas Nelson, Inc., 2008), 116-7

41. John 14:30 NLT

42. Lewis, *Yours, Jack*, 199

43. Rom. 8:12 NLT

44. Charles Haddon Spurgeon. *Morning and Evening*, 103

45. 1 John 1:9 NIV

46. Eph. 4:22-24 NLT

47. Rom. 12:1-2 NLT

48. Young, *Dear Jesus*, 128-9

49. Lewis, *Mere Christianity*, 94

50. *Cleansing Stream Seminar Workbook*, 3-20

51. Phil. 2:12-13 NIV

52. Zech. 4:6 NIV

53. Eph. 4:15-16 NIV

54. John 16;33 NIV

55. Exodus 23:30 NIV

56. Gerald G. May, M.D., *Will and Spirit: A Contemplative Psychology*, (New York, NY, Harper Collins Publishers, 1982), 118-119. I believe that all real truth is God's truth. Because I agree with May's observation that this is a danger, I quoted him. Using this quote is in no way an agreement with his view that all major spiritual traditions lead to core truths or to God. Isolated "nuggets" of truth can, in fact, exist in the writings and traditions of various religions. But, they can only be recognized by comparing them with Biblical truth.

57. Phil. 2:13 NIV

58. Keller, *The Reason for God*, 187

Chapter 8 - After Word

1. John 10:10 NIV

2. A wonderful discussion of these ideas can be found in chapter fourteen of Keller, *The Reason for God*, 222-236, THE DANCE OF GOD.

3. Phil. 4:19 NLT

4. Appendix C

5. Adapted from: Dr. Tim Clinton & Dr. Gary Sibcy, *Attachments: Why You Love, Feel, and Act the Way You Do*, (Nashville, TN: Thomas Nelson, Inc., 2002), Chester & Betsy Klystra, *Biblical Healing and Deliverance: A Guide to Experiencing Freedom*, (Grand Rapids, MI, Chosen Books,2005), 126-129, and strongholds that show up repeatedly with Christian Life Coaching clients.

www.ingramcontent.com/pod-product-compliance
Lightning Source LLC
Chambersburg PA
CBHW051146120626
46547CB00012B/971